# THE SENATE OF THE ROMAN REPUBLIC

## Addresses on the History of Roman Constitutionalism

ROBERT C. BYRD

United States Senator

U.S. Government Printing Office

Washington

103d Congress, 2d Session
S. Con. Res. 68
U.S. Senate

Senate Document 103–23
U.S. Government Printing Office
Washington: 1995

*cover design:*   Eagle with spread wings standing on thunderbolt, ROMA.
Gold coin, ca. 211–209 B.C. (14 mm., 3.42 gm.). British Museum.

**Library of Congress Cataloging in Publication Data**

Byrd, Robert C.
    The Senate of the Roman Republic : addresses on the history of Roman
constitutionalism / Robert C. Byrd.
        p.    cm.—(S. doc. ; 103–23)
    "103d Congress, 2d Session, S. Con. Res. 68, U.S. Senate"—T.p. verso.
    Includes bibliographical references.
    1. Rome.    Senate.    I. Title.    II. Series: Senate document (United
States. Congress. Senate) ; 103–23.
    JC85.S4B95      1994
    328.3'1'0937—dc20                                                94–38166
                                                                          CIP

For sale by the Superintendent of Documents
U.S. Government Printing Office
Washington, DC 20402

To Erma, My Wife

# Contents

# Illustrations

# Foreword

Skyrocketing budget deficits during the 1980's produced numerous legislative proposals to bring the federal budget under control. In 1982, the Senate passed a balanced budget constitutional amendment, but the House of Representatives failed to obtain the two-thirds vote necessary to send the proposal to the states. In 1985, resorting to statute rather than constitutional amendment, Congress passed the Balanced Budget and Emergency Deficit Control Act (Gramm-Rudman-Hollings) and renewed its provisions two years later, although this statute ultimately failed to achieve its objectives. In 1986, the Senate considered a second balanced budget amendment, but failed to pass it by a one-vote margin. In 1994, congressional supporters of a budget balancing amendment fell short by a small margin in both chambers. Proponents of structural budgetary constraints on Congress also renewed longstanding efforts to alter the Constitution by giving the president authority to veto individual items within appropriations bills.

On May 5, 1993, Senator Robert C. Byrd, chairman of the Senate Appropriations Committee, initiated a series of fourteen addresses in opposition to the proposed line-item-veto concept. *During the following five and a-half months, he delivered each of these speeches—packed with names, dates, and complex narratives—entirely from memory and without recourse even to notes or consultation with staff aides.* The first two sentences of his opening address offered the flavor of what was to come.

> Mr. President, twelve years of trickle-down, supply-side Reaganomics, Laffer curves, and a borrow-and-spend national credit card binge have left the country with a deteriorating infrastructure, a stagnant economy, high unemployment, triple-digit billion-dollar deficits, a $4 trillion debt, and a $200 billion annual interest payment on that debt.
>
> In search of antidotes for this fast-spreading fiscal melanoma of suffocating deficits and debts, the budget medicine men have once again begun their annual pilgrimage to the shrine of Saint Line-Item Veto, to worship at the altar of fool's gold, quack remedies—such as enhanced rescission, line-item veto, and other graven images—which, if adopted, would give rise to unwarranted expectations and possibly

[ix]

raise serious constitutional questions involving separation of powers, checks and balances, and control of the national purse.

Senator Byrd devised the equivalent of a fourteen-week university seminar on the constitutional history of separated and shared powers as shaped in the republic and empire of ancient Rome. To prepare himself for this task, the senior West Virginia senator read extensively on the history of England and ancient Rome. He began with the writings of Montesquieu, the eighteenth-century French philosopher who had also studied and thought deeply about the history of Rome and the operation of contemporary English governmental institutions. Montesquieu's political philosophy had profoundly influenced the thinking of those who framed the U.S. Constitution. To better understand what the framers had in mind when they created a governmental system of divided and shared powers, Senator Byrd carefully examined Montesquieu's 1734 essay, *Considerations on the Causes of the Greatness of the Romans and their Decline.*

Senator Byrd reasoned that, "if the history of the Roman people helped to influence Montesquieu's political philosophy concerning checks and balances and the separation of powers, and if Montesquieu's political theory influenced our American forebears in their writing of the United States Constitution, then why can it not be said that the history of Rome and the Romans, as well as the history of England and Englishmen, influenced [the Constitution's framers]." To test this premise, he examined the works of more than twenty celebrated historians of ancient Rome who wrote from the time of Polybius, in the second century before Christ, down through Sallust, Julius Caesar, Livy, Plutarch, Tacitus, Suetonius, and others, concluding with Edward Gibbon in the eighteenth century.

In his fourteen addresses, Senator Byrd described the development of ancient Rome from its legendary founding in 753 B.C., through its evolution to a republic with a strong and independent Senate and then into its decline and collapse as the Roman Senate willingly yielded hard-won powers to a succession of dictators and emperors.

The Roman Senate had emerged as the mainstay of an extended struggle against executive authority for power to control the purse. For centuries, the Senate of ancient Rome was made up of "the wisest, the best educated, the most respected, most experienced, most vigilant, most patriotic men of substance in the Roman republic." But "when the Roman Senate gave up its control of the purse strings, it gave away its power to check the executive. From that point on, the Senate declined. . . . Once the mainstay was weakened, the structure collapsed and the Roman republic fell."

Senator Byrd sees ample parallels between the willingness of Roman senators to hand over powers of the purse to usurping executives and the compliant attitude of United States senators in responding to presidential urging for a similar grant of powers in a line-item veto constitutional amendment. Taken together, this fourteen-part series displays vast learning, prodigious memory, and single-minded determination to preserve constitutional prerogatives forged over more than two millennia of human experience.

RICHARD A. BAKER
*Director*
U.S. Senate Historical Office

## Acknowledgements

For their accommodations and courtesies during the more than five months in 1993 when I delivered this series of one-hour speeches, I wish to thank the two leaders—Senator George Mitchell and Senator Robert Dole—and the floor staffs—Abby Saffold, Lula Davis, Martin Paone, Howard Greene, and Elizabeth Greene. I also appreciate the assistance of Dr. Richard Baker who encouraged me throughout this project.

ROBERT C. BYRD

# On the Senate of the Roman Republic

*The Roman Senate had complete control over the purse. It determined foreign policy, executed foreign policy, made and ratified treaties. It approved or disapproved legislation. It approved the elections of magistrates, and it determined who would be entrusted with the powers of dictator in a time of crisis for the Roman state. The Roman Senate was the guardian of the Roman state. It was the conscience of the republic. [page 161]*

❦

*[A] weakened Senate—once the resplendent and supreme pillar of power undergirding the rugged, yet graceful architecture of the Roman republic—had lost its way, its nerve, its vision, and its independence. The Roman Senate—for so many centuries the pride of the republic—had failed at the critical junctures to demonstrate the firmness, the considered judgment, and the integrity that might not only have arrested, but might also have reversed, the decline of the republic. [page 128]*

❦

*Gaius Julius Caesar did not seize power in Rome. The Roman Senate thrust power on Caesar deliberately with forethought, with surrender, with intent to escape from responsibility. The Senate gave away power; the members [of that body] . . . abandoned their duty as senators, and, in doing so, created in Caesar the most powerful man in the ancient world and one of the most powerful men in all history. [page 163]*

❦

*I am afraid we may be contemplating, with the line-item veto, the example of the Roman Senate: losing our nerve and shifting the power of the people, through their elected representatives, to an all-powerful executive. If we do that, then we, the senators and representatives of today, will be held accountable by our children and our children's children, just as history must hold the Roman Senate largely accountable, in the final analysis, for the decline and fall of the Roman republic. [page 81]*

# Chronology

| | |
|---|---|
| 445 | The Canuleian law gives patricians and plebeians right to intermarry. |
| 443 | Creation of the office of censor with power to remove senators for misconduct. |
| 390 | Capture of Rome by the Gauls under Brennus. |
| 367 | Licinian plebiscite provided that one of the two consuls elected annually must be a plebeian. |
| 343–341 | First Samnite War. |
| 327–304 | Second Samnite War. |
| 298–290 | Third Samnite War. |
| 287 | Hortensian Law. Plebiscites to be binding on all citizens, patricians as well as plebeians. |
| 280 | Battle of Heraclea. |
| 279 | Battle of Asculum. |
| 264–241 | First Punic War. |
| 218–202 | Second Punic War. |
| 218 | Battle at the Trebbia River. |
| 217 | Battle at Lake Trasimene. |
| 216 | Battle of Cannae. |
| 215–205 | First Macedonian War. |
| 207 | Battle at the Metaurus River. |
| 205 ca.–125 ca. | Polybius. |
| 202 | Battle of Zama. Hannibal defeated by Publius Cornelius Scipio Africanus Major. |
| 200–197 | Second Macedonian War. |
| 171–167 | Third Macedonian War. |
| 143–133 | Spanish Wars (Numantine). |
| 149–146 | Third Punic War. |

| | |
|---|---|
| 146 | Carthage destroyed by Publius Cornelius Scipio Aemilianus Africanus. Corinth destroyed by Mummius, thereby completing Roman conquest of Greece. |
| 133 | Tribunate of Tiberius Gracchus. Emergence of Optimates vs. Populares. |
| 123–122 | Tribunates of Gaius Gracchus. |
| 112–106 | The Jugurthine War. |
| 106 | Cicero born. |
| 100 | Julius Caesar born. |
| 90–88 | Social War (War against the Allies). |
| 88–86 | Rivalry of Marius and Sulla. |
| 88–84 | First Mithridatic War. |
| 86–84 | Sulla vs. Cinna. |
| 86–34 | Gaius Sallustius Crispus (Sallust). |
| 83–81 | Second Mithridatic War. |
| 82–81 | Dictatorship of Sulla (resigned dictatorship in 81 and became consul in 80). |
| 79 | Sulla retires/dies in 78 B.C. |
| 74–63 | Third Mithridatic War. |
| 73–71 | The war with Spartacus the Gladiator. |
| 67 | The Pirate War. Pompey triumphant. |
| 63–62 | The conspiracy of Catiline. |
| 60 | First Triumvirate (Pompey, Caesar, Crassus). |
| 59 | First consulship of Caesar. |
| 59–51 | Caesar's Gallic Wars. |
| 59–17 A.D. | Titus Livius (Livy). |
| 55 | Caesar invades Britain. |
| 53 | Death of Crassus at Carrhae. |
| 49 | Caesar crosses the Rubicon. |

| | |
|---|---|
| 49–44 | Caesar's dictatorships. |
| 48 | Battle of Pharsalus. Pompey killed in Egypt. |
| 47 | Battle of Zela. Caesar defeats Pharnaces II. |
| 46 | Battle of Thapsus. Cato the Younger commits suicide. |
| 45 | Battle of Munda. |
| 44 | Caesar assassinated. |
| 43 | Cicero killed. Second Triumvirate (Antony, Lepidus, Octavianus). |
| 42 | Battles of Philippi. Brutus and Cassius commit suicide. |
| 31 | Battle of Actium. Antony and Cleopatra defeated by Octavius. Final collapse of Roman republic. |
| 30 | Antony and Cleopatra commit suicide. |
| 27 | Senate confers title of Augustus on Octavian. |
| 23 | Birth of Roman empire. |
| 19 B.C.–30 A.D. | Velleius Paterculus. |

—A.D.—

| | |
|---|---|
| 46 ca.–120 ca. | Mestrius Plutarchus (Plutarch). |
| 55 ca.–120 ca. | Cornelius Tacitus. |
| 70–140 | Gaius Suetonius Tranquillus (Suetonius). |
| 155 ca.–240 ca. | Dio Cassius Cocceianus. |
| 385–418 | Paulus Orosius. |
| 500 ca.–565 ca. | Procopius. |
| 1689–1755 | Charles-Louis de Secondat, baron de la Brède et de Montesquieu. |
| 1734 | Montesquieu's *Considerations on the Causes of the Greatness of the Romans and their Decline* published anonymously. |

| 1737–1794 | Edward Gibbon. |
| 1776–1788 | Gibbon's *The History of the Decline and Fall of the Roman Empire* published. |
| 1787 | U.S. Constitution drafted in Philadelphia. Article I, Section 1, provides, "All legislative Powers herein granted shall be vested in a Congress of the United States, which shall consist of a Senate and House of Representatives." Article I, Section 9, provides, "No Money shall be drawn from the Treasury, but in Consequence of Appropriations made by Law;" |
| 1789 | United States Senate convenes for the first time. |

# In the Senate of the United States

_January 7_, 1959

I, _Robert C. Byrd_, do solemnly swear (or affirm) that I will support and defend the Constitution of the United States against all enemies, foreign and domestic; that I will bear true faith and allegiance to the same; that I take this obligation freely, without any mental reservation or purpose of evasion; and that I will well and faithfully discharge the duties of the office on which I am about to enter: So help me God.

_Robert C. Byrd_

Subscribed and sworn to before me this _7th_ day of _January_, A. D. 1959

_Richard Nixon_
President of the Senate.

State _West Virginia_

Oath of Office

# CHAPTER 1

# We Have a Solemn Covenant

*May 5, 1993*

Mr. BYRD. Mr. President, twelve years of trickle-down, supply-side Reaganomics, Laffer curves, and a borrow-and-spend national credit card binge have left the country with a deteriorating infrastructure, a stagnant economy, high unemployment, triple-digit billion-dollar deficits, a $4 trillion debt, and a $200 billion annual interest payment on that debt.

In search of antidotes for this fast-spreading fiscal melanoma of suffocating deficits and debt, the budget medicine men have once again begun their annual pilgrimage to the shrine of Saint Line-Item Veto, to worship at the altar of fool's gold, quack remedies—such as enhanced rescission, line-item veto, and other graven images—which, if adopted, would give rise to unwarranted expectations and possibly raise serious constitutional questions involving separation of powers, checks and balances, and control of the national purse.

Congressional appropriations are always the target of these patent medicines, these misguided efforts. In referring to them as misguided efforts, I do not impugn the good intentions of many people outside the Congress and many people inside the Congress in both houses.

Many of these individuals honestly believe that this is the way to go in order to control the bloated deficits that have us drowning in a sea of red ink. On the other hand, Mr. President, some of these people inside Congress, and outside Congress, who constantly press for the line-item veto, enhanced rescissions, or other quack nostrums, know, or ought to know, that these are nothing more than placebos, spurious magic incantations, witch's brew, and various brands of snake oil remedies.

They ought to know better. Plutarch wrote that Menestheus, regent of Athens, was said to be the first of mankind to undertake to be a demagog, and by his eloquence to ingratiate himself with the people.

In recent years, Mr. President, especially since the big triple-digit, billion-dollar deficits became an annual occurrence here in Washington, beginning with the first Reagan administration, we have seen a seeming plethora of demagogs. Mr. Reagan himself was one of the foremost disciples of the theory that the line-item veto would be a cure-all for these bloated deficits; and Mr. Bush followed quickly in his train.

I would not say that this seeming spate of demagogic characters has sprung like Aphrodite from the ocean foam, or like Minerva from the forehead of Jove. They just seem to come in litters. Every year we are treated to this spectacle of attempts to make us believe that the line-item veto would be a painless cure, which would rid the country of its fiscal headaches and provide a sure and painless ticket to a blissful Utopian paradise that would be debt free, deficit free, and care free.

There are people in this chamber and in the other body who, I am sure, honestly believe that this is the way to go. They believe in their hearts that the line-item veto or enhanced rescissions would be the sure and painless medicine by which these deficits can be brought under control and kept under control. But there are others who appear to be making a political career of preying upon the unknowing, unsuspecting, and suffering public for political and partisan gain.

Mr. President, the deficit problem is not caused by congressional appropriations. Since 1945, and through last year, beginning with Truman, and following with Eisenhower, Kennedy, Johnson, Nixon, Ford, Carter, Reagan, and Bush, the total appropriations—supplementals, regular, and deficiencies—have amounted to $200,848,154,902 less than the totality of all the budget requests that these nine presidents have submitted during all those years.

Discretionary domestic spending is what is most often mentioned by ultracrepidarian critics, who refer to it as congres-

[2]

sional "pork", but which is, indeed, infrastructure. But domestic discretionary appropriations have not created the budget deficits. The deficit problem is much broader, much bigger than this. It has been brought on by a combination of practices, such as mandatory back-door spending, tax expenditures, costly programmatic initiatives that come from authorizing committees, and the force-feeding of the military-industrial complex about which President Eisenhower so eloquently spoke as he was completing his tenure of office.

### Standing the Legislative Process on its Head

The question is, can we develop a way whereby a president— not just President Clinton, not just a Democratic president, any president—working with the Congress, can get better control over spending. I am referring not just to appropriations, but also to other types of spending. Keep in mind that the appropriations committees have control only over about a third of the total budget. It will not be easy. It is a very complex problem, and it will require a great deal of thought and effort to make this come about, if indeed it can be made to come about.

Only last week the House passed a bill, and the bill has been received in the Senate. That bill provides that the president may, within three calendar days following the enactment of an appropriations bill, send to the House of Representatives a message and a bill incorporating rescissions which he would suggest be made. The House of Representatives, within a very few calendar days, would be required to introduce the president's bill and send it to the appropriations committee of the House. In a very short time span the appropriations committee of the House would be required to report that bill, or it would be considered to be automatically reported, together with a committee substitute. Then, under a very short time limitation for debate, something like four hours in the House, the House would be expected to pass the president's bill and send it to the Senate. If the House rejected the president's bill, then it would take up the Appropriations Committee's complete substitute. The House then would vote on the substitute, presumably pass that substitute, and send it to the Senate.

[3]

In either case, whether the president's bill or the House Appropriations Committee's substitute were passed by the House and sent to the Senate, that bill or that substitute would be sent to the Senate Appropriations Committee. The Senate Appropriations Committee would have only a very few days in which to report that legislation to the Senate.

The Senate Appropriations Committee would be required to report the House measure without substantive change, along with its own substitute. Then the Senate would take up the House measure first; if it is rejected, the Senate would take up the Senate Appropriations Committee substitute. All this is to be done within ten hours of Senate floor debate.

Mr. President, it boggles the imagination to try to comprehend just how such a measure came to be put together in the House of Representatives. I do not question for a moment the good intentions of the House members; they could have sent worse to the Senate, I suppose. But it has all the makings of a bill that was totally put together during debate on the floor of the House of Representatives.

I compliment the House leadership on both sides of the aisle and the House members for at least making the effort; they tried to do something. But what we have pending in the Senate now is a House measure that stands the legislative process on its head. Instead of voting on amendments first and then on the bill, the House and Senate would vote on the bill first and, if it were rejected, they then would vote on a substitute amendment. No amendments would be in order from the floor of either body. It is, simply, a take-it-or-leave-it situation. Take the president's bill in the House, or, if that bill is rejected, take the committee substitute in its entirety from the House Appropriations Committee, but with no amendments from the floor.

In the Senate, we must accept either the president's bill or a committee substitute that is sent over from the House, refer it to the Senate Appropriations Committee, and then bring it back without substantive change, accompanied only by a Senate Appropriations Committee substitute. Debate on the Senate floor would be limited to ten hours, with no floor amendments in order. The Senate would be limited to an up-or-down vote on a House-passed vehicle, and if that were rejected,

[4]

the Senate would be then limited to an up-or-down vote on the Senate committee substitute—and I repeat, with no floor amendments in order.

Mr. President, I wonder what we have come to in this body, if the Senate of the United States is mandated to take up a matter of such importance, debate it in a very short time period which can be further reduced by a nondebatable motion approved by a majority, and required to act without any amendments from the floor.

I cannot conceive of senators in 1959—when I first came to the Senate—accepting this kind of a proposal. Of course, we did not have such massive deficits back then. That was before the trickle-down, supply-side theory of Reaganomics hit Washington like a storm. But even so, I cannot picture those senators accepting a legislative approach in which the Senate would be bound and gagged and unable to offer amendments from the floor. And, as a matter of fact, the House measure says that that provision cannot even be changed by unanimous consent. No unanimous-consent request would be in order in either body to allow amendments from the floor.

Is today's Senate going to accept this kind of a gag proposition? I wonder. I wonder.

### THE WISEST OF THE WISE

Mr. President, the Roman Senate, as originally created, was meant to be made up of a body of old men; not the swiftest of the swift, nor the strongest of the strong, but the wisest of the wise. That is the reason why they were to be old men. They were to have had the experience of a lifetime, with lessons learned in the hard school of experience for their guidance. And so Romulus, the legendary founder of Rome, created a Senate of old men, one hundred noblemen.

I suppose that one who has lived as long as I have—God has so blessed me with a long life beyond the psalmist's span—can look back over a lifetime of seventy-five years and in that time will have gained some wisdom from experience—perhaps only a little; perhaps much. Some people, after seventy-five years, will be more wise than others; some perhaps not wise at all.

[5]

But if one is to gain in wisdom by virtue of his long years of life, how much more will he gain in wisdom if he studies the lives of great men? If he studies history as it bridges the centuries of time, he then becomes the recipient, the beneficiary of the wisdom of hundreds of lifetimes stretching back into the dim mists of antiquity. That is why we are told to study history.

Cicero, a great Roman senator, said that one "ought to be acquainted with the history of the events of past ages. To be ignorant of what occurred before you were born is to remain always a child. For what is the worth of human life unless it is woven into the life of our ancestors by the records of history?"

Machiavelli, writing in *The Prince,* advised the prince to study history; to study the victories and defeats of others so that one might gain therefrom and achieve the one or avoid the other, and to emulate some great person as Alexander the Great did Achilles, as Caesar did Alexander the Great, or as Scipio did Cyrus the Great.

Well, I took Cicero's words to heart quite a long time ago and I have attempted to look at history, ancient history as well as the history of England and American history. I have attempted, through several years of patient and laborious study, to get a broad view of history. Herodotus, who lived between the years circa 484 and 424 B.C., wrote about the Persian empire of Cyrus the Great, Cambyses, Darius the Great, and Xerxes. Thucydides—the Athenian commander who was exiled for twenty years because he failed to come to the relief of Amphipolis against Brasidas, the brilliant Spartan general— picked up in his history where Herodotus left off.

Thucydides was a man who saw more clearly, inquired more responsibly, and reported more honestly than most other ancient historians. He lived between the years circa 460 and 400 B.C. Xenophon (434-355 B.C.), a student of Socrates, picked up in his history where Thucydides left off. Xenophon's *Anabasis* describes the expedition of Cyrus the Younger into Persia— the expedition and then the retreat after the battle of Cunaxa, which took place in 401 B.C. Xenophon, who, following the battle, was elected general by the ten thousand Greek mercenaries, wrote the history of that terrible retreat which required

[6]

about eight months and covered a distance of about 1,650 miles.

Mr. President, let us now turn to a consideration of the renowned French philosopher and writer, Montesquieu. Montesquieu had a great impact upon our constitutional framers. They were very conversant with the English experience, the long struggle for liberty by Englishmen against tyrannical monarchs. They were also well versed in the political theory and philosophy of Montesquieu. Montesquieu was born one hundred years before the first Senate met. He was born in 1689; died in 1755, just thirty-two years before our constitutional forebears met in Philadelphia in 1787. They were very cognizant of his political theory.

Montesquieu believed that the judicial, executive, and legislative powers should be separated. If they were kept separated, the result would be political freedom, because the checks and balances would act, one against the other. But if these various powers were concentered in one man, as in his native France, then the result would be tyranny.

Montesquieu visited the more important and larger political divisions of Europe and spent a considerable time in England. His extensive English connections had a tremendous influence on the development of his political philosophy.

We are acquainted with his *Spirit of the Laws* and with his *Persian Letters*, but perhaps we are not so familiar with the fact that he also wrote a philosophical analysis of the history of the Romans and the Roman state. And it is, I think, quite accurate to say that contemporary English institutions and the history of Rome, more decisively than anything else, influenced the general system of Montesquieu's political theory and philosophy.

Therefore, if one is to better understand the principles and theory of our own Constitution, one should be familiar with Montesquieu's political thought and, following in Montesquieu's tracks, also study Roman history.

Montesquieu, in 1734, produced his essay, *Considerations on the Causes of the Greatness of the Romans and their Decline*. If Rome and the state system of the Romans and the history of the Roman people helped to influence Montesquieu's political philosophy concerning checks and balances and the separation

[7]

of powers, and if Montesquieu's political theory influenced our American forebears in their writing of the United States Constitution, then why can it not be said that the history of Rome and the Romans, as well as the history of England and Englishmen, influenced our forefathers as they sat, in the summer of 1787, in Philadelphia and hammered out this marvelous document, the United States Constitution?

### SENATORS TAKE AN OATH

We take a solemn oath to support and defend the Constitution every time we are sworn in as new members and as members who are reelected. I have taken that oath as a senator six times. As the Senate president pro tempore, I have administered that oath many times to other senators.

Mr. President, as I have attempted to evaluate and analyze these questions of separation of powers, checks and balances, line-item veto, enhanced rescissions, expedited rescissions, and the control over the national purse, I have wondered if we senators really think much about our oath of office. I wonder if, during the six years following our being sworn into office, we give any further thought to that oath, to its meaning, and to the responsibilities and duties that devolve upon us by virtue of our having sworn to that oath in the presence of our colleagues, with our hand on the Bible, and repeating the closing words of the oath, "So help me God."

As I have sat here these last few years, and have witnessed the attacks made upon Congress, upon the legislative process, upon the appropriations process, upon the Constitution and its checks and balances and separation of powers, I am made to wonder just how much we senators really think about the oath that we took when we were sworn into office. It is easy to judge others, and it is easy to be wrong in one's judgment of others. But I am constrained to wonder, as we often vote on such matters, just how much we really stop and reflect on the solemn oath that we take to support and defend the Constitution of the United States against all enemies, foreign and domestic.

We know a great deal about the history of Rome, the Roman Senate, and ancient oaths—thanks to the writings of a remarkable succession of historians over an eight-hundred-year span,

[8]

from Polybius in the second century before Christ through Procopius in the sixth century A.D. Many of these historians were contemporary observers of the events they so richly described. I have spent hundreds of hours reading the massive library of works by these great historians to prepare myself for the series of addresses that will follow this one.*

Let us, for example, consult Polybius—who was present at the final destruction of Carthage in 146 B.C.—on the subject of the Roman oath. "Among the Romans, whether in accounting for public or private funds, the people are trustworthy because of the oath they have taken." Montesquieu said that, when it came to the oath, "the Romans were the most religious people in the world" because that oath "always formed the nerve of their military discipline."

The ancient Romans took the oath seriously. Lucius Junius Brutus, who, after the rule by kings of 243 years, became one of the first two consuls, along with Collatinus Tarquinius, made the Roman people swear an oath that never again would they subject themselves to the rule of kings. Lucius Junius Brutus was reputed to be the great, great ancestor of Marcus Junius Brutus, who participated in the assassination of Caesar.

Lucius Junius Brutus, when he later learned that his own two sons, Titus and Tiberius, were participating in a conspiracy

---

*These historians include: Polybius, ca.205–ca.125 B.C., *Histories*; Diodorus of Sicily, late first century B.C., *Historical Library*; Dionysius of Halicarnassus, died ca.7 B.C., *Roman Antiquities*; Cornelius Nepos, first century B.C., *Vitae Excellentium Imperatorum*; Gaius Sallustius Crispus (Sallust), 86–34 B.C., *History of the Jugurthine War* and *Conspiracy of Cataline*; Julius Caesar, 100–44 B.C., *The Gallic Wars*; Titus Livius (Livy), 59 B.C.–17 A.D., *The Annals of the Roman People*; Gnaeus Pompeius Trogus, first century B.C. to first century A.D., an abridged general history of Rome; Mestrius Plutarchus (Plutarch), ca.46–ca.120 A.D., *Parallel Lives*; Cornelius Tacitus, ca.55–ca.120 A.D., *Historiae, Dialogus de oratoribus, De vita Julii Agricolae, De origine et situ Germanorum, Annales*; Gaius Suetonius Tranquillus (Suetonius), 70–140 A.D., *Lives of the Caesars*; Flavius Arrianus (Arrian), second century A.D., *Anabasis of Alexander* and *Periplus of the Euxine*; Appianus (Appian), second century A.D., *Romaika*; Lucius Annaeus Florus, early second century A.D., outline history of Rome; Dio Cassius Cocceianus, ca.155–ca.240 A.D., a history of Rome, nine volumes; Flavius Eutropius, fourth century A.D., *Breviarium ab Urbe Condita*; Ammianus Marcellinus, second half of the fourth century A.D., a history of the Roman empire from 96–378 A.D. (a continuation of Tacitus' history); Orosius, 385–418 A.D.; Zosimus, fifth century A.D., a history of Rome from the early emperors to the capture of Rome by Alaric in 410; Procopius, ca.500–565 A.D., *Histories*; and, one of the greatest of all historians, Edward Gibbon, 1737–1794, *The History of the Decline and Fall of the Roman Empire*. I found the following two modern works particularly helpful: Will Durant, *Caesar and Christ, A History of Roman Civilization and of Christianity from their Beginnings to A.D. 325* (Volume 3 in his *Story of Civilization* series, 1944) and Arthur E. R. Boak and William G. Sinnigen, *A History of Rome to A.D. 565*, fifth edition (1965).

to bring back the Etruscan kings, had his two sons executed because they had broken their oath and proved to be traitors. Such was the solemnity of the Roman oath.

### THE CONSTITUTION: PRODUCT OF EXPERIENCE, KNOWLEDGE, AND HISTORY

Mr. President, over the next few days and weeks, I shall focus on Roman history so that we might better understand, from a broader perspective, that our own political system of separation of powers and checks and balances did not spring full-blown in 1787 from the brains of those men who framed our Constitution at Philadelphia. Indeed, our Constitution was the product of experience, knowledge, and history. The Framers had a broad perspective. And that is what I hope that we, in our time, will seek to achieve: a broad perspective, so that we can better focus upon and revere this Constitution and the origins of its separation of powers and checks and balances. We need to consider how they came into being and what they mean for us. We must not just look at them through the narrow prism of contemporary polls, or with a narrow focus on political and partisan gain, and, like demagogs, succumb to the "Alcibiades syndrome." (Alcibiades was a young Athenian politician in the fifth century B.C. with a silver tongue, who placed his own personal and political interests ahead of the national interests.)

I am afraid that we, all of us, from time to time are infected with the Alcibiades syndrome, putting our own selfish personal, political, partisan interests ahead of the national interests, ahead of the public interests. As we approach the time when the Senate majority leader may call up the House bill on expedited rescissions, I want us to focus more on the folly of such a perverted process and to back off from it just a little bit and see the forest as well as the trees. I think if we do this, we will know more than we now know, and we will be better able to reflect upon just what our duty is in today's Senate.

Aaron Burr, on March 2, 1805, after he had served four years as vice president of the United States, upon leaving the presiding officer's chair in the old chamber down the hall, made a speech to the Senate as he prepared to depart therefrom for the last time. It was a speech that gripped the attention of senators. We are told that for several minutes after the doors had closed behind him, senators were speechless, some of them in tears.

Burr, in a duel, had murdered Alexander Hamilton at Weehawken, New Jersey, in July 1804, and had just presided over the Senate impeachment trial of Supreme Court Justice Samuel Chase. At the close of his speech, Burr said this:

> This House is a sanctuary; a citadel of law, of order, and of liberty; and it is here—it is here, in this exalted refuge; here, if anywhere, will resistance be made to the storms of political phrensy and the silent arts of corruption; and if the Constitution be destined ever to perish by the sacrilegious hands of the demagogue or the usurper, which God avert, its expiring agonies will be witnessed on this floor.

Mr. President, if the Senate ever takes up this House-passed expedited rescissions bill, and if it were to adopt this measure, the Senate would thereby deprive itself of its freedom and prerogative to offer amendments, and it would surrender power over the purse to the executive. I wonder if this perhaps may not be the culmination of the prophecy by Burr. To me, it is such a profoundly serious matter—not because I am chairman of the Appropriations Committee, but because the bill threatens the equilibrium of powers established by the Constitution.

I have a reverence for the legislative branch under the Constitution, a reverence for the separation of powers and checks and balances of the Constitution, a reverence for history.

Tacitus said, "Think of your ancestors and your descendants as you go into battle." We have a covenant with the past. We have a covenant with our forebears, who were willing to pledge their lives, their fortunes, and their sacred honor for us.

We also have a covenant with the future—our children and grandchildren. We have a covenant, both with the past and with the future.

Mr. President, we may be about to break that covenant with the past and with the future. When the decision time comes, hopefully, we will remember our oath of office and reflect on our covenant with our ancestors and our descendants.

[11]

We cannot ignore that covenant, Mr. President. We cannot take it lightly. We are links in a vital chain both to the dead and to the unborn. We are, at one and the same time, the sons of sires who sleep in calm assurance that we will not betray the trust that they confided to our hands; and the sires of sons who wait confident, in the beyond, that we will not cheat them of their birthright.

I close, therefore, in the spirit of those immortal lines by Kipling:

> Our fathers in a wondrous age
>     Ere yet the Earth was small,
> Ensured to us an heritage
>     And doubted not at all
> That we, the children of their heart,
>     Which then did beat so high,
> In later time should play like part
>     For our posterity.
>
> Then fretful murmur not they gave
>     So great a charge to keep,
> Nor dream that awestruck time shall save
>     Their labour while we sleep.
> Dear-bought and clear, a thousand year
>     Our fathers' title runs;
> Make we likewise their sacrifice,
>     Defrauding not our sons.

*But as to exercise for the mind, the prince ought to read history and study the actions of eminent men, see how they acted in warfare, examine the causes of their victories and defeats in order to imitate the former and avoid the latter, and above all, do as some men have done in the past, who have imitated someone, who has been much praised and glorified, and have always kept his deeds and actions before them, as they say Alexander the Great imitated Achilles; Caesar, Alexander; and Scipio, Cyrus. And whoever reads the life of Cyrus written by Xenophon, will perceive in the life of Scipio how gloriously he imitated the former, and how, in chastity, affability, humanity, and liberality, Scipio conformed to those qualities of Cyrus as described by Xenophon.*

Machiavelli, *The Prince*

෪෪

*When the legislative and executive powers are united in the same person, or in the same body of magistrates, there can be no liberty; because apprehensions may arise, lest the same monarch or senate should enact tyrannical laws, to execute them in a tyrannical manner.*

Montesquieu, *The Spirit of the Laws*

[13]

*Charles Louis de Secondat, baron de la Brède et de Montesquieu*

# CHAPTER 2

# The Roman State System Develops

*May 11, 1993*

Mr. BYRD. Mr. President, the line-item veto was included in the Constitution of the Confederate States of America. It was first proposed at the federal level by President Ulysses Grant in 1873, and three years later, in 1876, the first resolution to amend the Constitution to provide the president of the United States with the line-item veto was introduced in the House of Representatives by none other than a representative from the State of West Virginia, Charles James Faulkner. Since that time, scores of such resolutions have been introduced in both bodies.

Last week I spoke of the line-item veto and other quick fixes, and I stated that, through the twelve years of the Reagan and Bush administrations and continuing to today, these popular fixes—I should call them expediencies—have been and continue to be advanced as cure-alls for the bloated budgets that have us drowning in a sea of red ink.

I stated last Wednesday that we have a responsibility as members of the Senate and members of the House to examine these popular expediencies through the broader context of hundreds of years of history which preceded the brilliant work of the constitutional framers in 1787 who established the counterweights of checks and balances in our constitutional system.

We also have a duty to remember our solemn oath to protect and defend this delicate constitutional structure.

I spoke on last Wednesday of a covenant that we have with the past—the dead who have gone on before us—and

[15]

the covenant that we have with the yet unborn, who will reap the harvest that we leave behind.

I said that it is a solemn covenant—it is not one to be taken lightly—and that we have a duty to honor that covenant, a duty to those of the past who now sleep in calm assurance that we will not betray the confidence that they have placed in our hands, and a covenant with the future, those who wait in the beyond, confident that we will not cheat them of their birthright.

Mr. President, my purpose in making these speeches is to sound a note of caution and to jar us out of the complacency of focusing our attention solely on the immediate. For if we, as a nation, and if we, as senators, succumb to the nearsightedness of only that which is imminent, and the egoism of only that which affects us personally, then, Mr. President, we are surely lost.

I spoke of that great author-philosopher Montesquieu, who was greatly influenced by the history of the contemporary institutions of his time in England and by the history of the ancient Roman people. He wrote a famous essay on the greatness and decline of the Romans.

It is commonly believed that his knowledge of Roman history and his recognition of, and belief in, the institutions of England, most influenced him in his development of political theory. This was a political theory that our forefathers who wrote the Constitution subscribed to. That theory was that the three powers—judicial, executive, and legislative—should be kept separate and distinct from one another to ensure political freedom. If those three powers were lodged in one individual, as in France, it was Montesquieu's belief that the result would be tyranny.

A NECESSARILY ABRIDGED CAPSULATION OF ROMAN HISTORY

Mr. President, I believe that we should examine the history of these great people, these very remarkable people, the early Romans, and their extraordinary state system which so influenced Montesquieu, and, through him, influenced the framers of the American Constitution.

This will, necessarily, have to be a brief and very abridged capsulation of Roman history as it is brought to bear upon

[16]

our discussions of separation of powers and of checks and balances—the supreme pillar upon which the constitutional system of our country rests. I will discuss only a few events which constitute milestones, as it were, in the history of the Roman people and which will emphasize those extraordinary factors in Roman life that should be of importance to us today, as we see our own republic deteriorating. I shall discuss the things that made the Romans the foremost people of their time and made the Roman republic the foremost republic of ancient times.

National pride led the Romans to connect their history with the history of the Greek world and led them to forge links with Greek mythology. Tradition, therefore, developed the legend of the flight of Aeneas from Troy with his father, Anchises, and his son, Ascanius, who founded the ancient city of Alba Longa in Italy in circa 1152 B.C., the legendary birthplace of Romulus and Remus, and from which Rome was an offshoot. Thus evolved the foundation stories which attributed a Trojan origin to the Romans through Aeneas, and attributed to his descendents, Romulus and Remus, the founding of Rome in 753 B.C.

Tradition has it that the twin brothers, Romulus and Remus, were set afloat in a basket on the river Tiber by their mother, Rhea Silvia, she having been so commanded by the king, King Amulius.

The basket was later found by the keeper of the royal flock, Faustulus, who took the twins from the basket and gave them to his wife, Larentia, to rear. In due time, Romulus and Remus decided to found a city, and they agreed that the gods should determine by augury for whom the city would be named and who would govern the city.

Remus was the first to observe six vultures flying overhead, and he accepted this as an augury from the gods. Romulus, waiting on another of the seven hills of Rome, later saw twelve vultures. Each, therefore, laid claim to the kingship—Remus, by virtue of his having priority, in seeing the augury first; Romulus, by virtue of his having seen double the amount of vultures in the augury. Incidentally, throughout the long history of Rome, it was believed that the twelve vultures indicated that Rome would exist for twelve centuries. And,

[17]

indeed, the western seat of the Roman empire existed 1,229 years, from 753 B.C. to 476 A.D.

### First King Creates Senate

The followers of each, Romulus and Remus, laid claim to the kingship. There developed a contention between the two, and Romulus, in a fit of anger, slew his brother Remus. The city was named after Romulus and he became the first king. He ruled from 753 to 716 B.C. He created a Senate with a membership of one hundred of the leaders of the top families, the clans. The purpose of the Senate was to advise Romulus, the king, and to aid him in the administration of the city.

Romulus eventually determined that the men, who had come from various areas in the nearby region, needed wives, and he, upon the advice of the Senate, sent embassies to the neighboring tribes to see if they would enter into an alliance and be willing to have their women intermarry with the men of Rome.

The neighboring tribes rejected these embassies, whereupon, according to tradition, Romulus invited the Sabines to partici-pate in certain games in honor of Neptune. During the games, at a given signal, the Romans seized the maidens of the Sabines and carried them away. There then developed a war between the Sabines and the Romans, but, by that time, the wives of the Romans had become attached to their Roman men and pleaded with their fathers and brothers and husbands to stop the war and live at peace. The two contending peoples did that. The Sabines, however, felt that they ought to have someone who would share the sovereignty with King Romulus. There-fore, Titus Tatius, a Sabine, was chosen and for a while those two men worked and ruled together in peace and harmony. Ultimately, however, Titus Tatius was killed by a mob, and Romulus once again became the sole ruler of Rome until the year 716. As tradition would have it, in a severe storm he was enveloped in a cloud and, during a great clap of thunder, was swept up into heaven.

The Romans were without a king for about a year because the senators could not decide on a successor. Finally, the people demanded that there must be a king. The Roman Senate told the people that they could select a king but that that person

[ 18 ]

would become king only if the Senate stamped its imprimatur upon him. The plebeians—the people generally—thought that this was a very gracious act upon the part of the Senate, but they insisted that the senators should select the king. The Sabines felt that they ought to have a king, since their own Titus Tatius had been dead for some time. There was at that time a very pious and just Sabine by the name of Numa Pompilius, and the people accepted the Senate's selection of Numa Pompilius as king, who reigned from 715—one year having elapsed as an interregnum following the death of Romulus—to 672 B.C.

Numa Pompilius, being the religious and just man that he was, thought that the Romans should be imbued with a respect and reverence for the gods. He pretended, therefore, to have nocturnal meetings with Egeria, a nymph goddess of water. From her, he pretended, as he came back to his people, to have received instructions as to the priesthood and the establishment of religious rituals. Numa Pompilius then proceeded to establish the priesthoods, the rituals, and the ceremonies to be conducted in worship of the various and sundry gods. He appointed vestal virgins to carry out the vestal service, provided a stipend for them, and decreed that they should maintain their virginity throughout their service.

From the beginning, therefore, the Roman people were imbued with a reverence for providence; theirs were pagan gods, but they believed that these gods had an interest in their destiny and that it was their purpose, as a people, to fulfill and carry forward that destiny of the Roman state.

Upon the death of Numa Pompilius in 672, the people elected, and the Senate confirmed, the next king, Tullus Hostilius. He taught the Romans military arts. He also built a Senate house for the one hundred members of the Senate, and he led the Romans in their frequent wars with neighboring tribes. Tullus Hostilius reigned until 640 B.C.

Ancus Marcius was then chosen king and reigned from 640 to 616 B.C. He built the first bridge across the Tiber. He also constructed the first prison in the city. When he died, Lucius Tarquinius Priscus, an Etruscan, became king. He reigned from 616 to 578 and was a good king. He increased the Senate membership to two hundred. He also undertook to build a

[19]

wall around the unfortified sections of the city and built sewers that led down to the Tiber. He was the first to make a political speech in the effort to sway the multitude, he being the first to campaign for the kingship.

Upon the death of Tarquinius Priscus in 578, Servius Tullius was named king by the people and confirmed by the Senate. The people chose, but the Senate had to ratify their choice for it to become effective. Here, then, was a primordial form of separation of powers and checks and balances—the people chose but the Senate could approve or disapprove.

Servius Tullius instituted the first census among the Romans, and he reigned from 578 to 534. Then, the last of the seven kings, Lucius Tarquinius Superbus, or Tarquin the Proud, became king and reigned from 534 to 510 B.C. He was the first king to disregard the advice of the Senate. He decided capital cases by himself without advice, thus striking terror among the population. He executed a good many of the senators. Sitting as the sole judge in civil and criminal cases, he was in a position to exile or to execute people, or to declare forfeit their lands and properties. In this way, he was able to plunder, and enrich himself.

Ultimately, his son, Sextus Tarquinius, raped Lucretia, the wife of Tarquinius Collatinus. Shakespeare writes about this crime in "The Rape of Lucrece." Lucretia, after telling her father and her husband, Collatinus, about the crime perpetrated by Sextus Tarquinius, committed suicide. Lucius Junius Brutus, a friend of Tarquinius Collatinus, rallied the people around himself and, in 510 B.C., drove Tarquin the Proud out of Rome, together with all of his family. Sextus Tarquinius was eventually slain.

RULE OF KINGS ENDED; CONSULS CHOSEN

For a year, there was no ruler of the Roman people. Lucius Junius Brutus, the first to be chosen as consul, made the Roman people swear that they would never again submit to the rule of kings. As consul, he increased the Senate's membership to three hundred. With him was chosen a colleague, Tarquinius Collatinus. They were the first two Roman consuls. Each could serve for one year. Each was given the Imperium—the supreme command over civil, administrative, and military affairs.

[20]

Each consul had twelve lictors. The lictors were men, usually of the lower class, who preceded the consul and cleared the way for him. They executed his orders and put people to death in the event that the consul decreed such an execution. The lictors carried a bundle of rods made of elm or birch, and in the midst of these rods were axes to indicate the supreme authority of the officer having the Imperium. These were called fasces. Later on, when praetors were created, each of them had only six lictors. When the office of dictator was created, he had twenty-four lictors, signifying that his command was supreme, even over the consuls.

Here, again, we see developing a check and balance. Each consul had equal authority with the other consul. Each consul could veto the actions of the other consul, and each consul could only serve one year. The early Romans were determined that no person would ever again become such a power as to equal that of a king.

There were, therefore, these checks and balances between the two consuls, and all other magistrates were subordinate to them. The consuls carried out the recommendations of the Roman Senate, expressed through what was called a *senatus consultum*. It did not have the formal title of law, but, de facto, it was the same as law.

Tarquin the Proud, having been driven from Rome, solicited the support of Lars Porsena, an Etruscan king of Clusium, in restoring himself, Lucius Tarquinius Superbus, to the kingship of Rome. Lars Porsena came with a great army and started to cross the Sublician Bridge across the Tiber. Horatius Cocles, one of the foremost of the Roman military men, stood on the bridge with two companions and withstood the attacks of this Etruscan army, urging, meanwhile, that the Romans destroy the bridge behind him so that the Etruscan army could not get across the river.

The bridge was destroyed, and Horatius Cocles plunged into the river and swam to safety. This is the subject of one of Macaulay's lays of ancient Rome. This event occurred somewhere between 509 B.C. and 500 B.C.

The Romans were divided into two distinct classes, the patricians and the plebeians. The patricians held all the seats of authority and the offices in the priesthood, as well as member-

[21]

ship in the Senate. And for a long time, the patricians' sons inherited their Senate seats.

But the patricians and the plebeians had an ongoing contention, the plebeians feeling offended, for one thing, in that intermarriage between patricians and plebeians was forbidden. The patricians held all of the important offices of authority in the military, in the civil administration, and in the Senate. They were the wealthy class. Yet, the plebeians helped to do the fighting in time of war, furnishing most of the soldiers. Whether one served in the military depended upon whether or not he owned property. Consequently, his voting in the Comitia Curiata and, later, the Comitia Centuriata, depended upon his ownership of property as well.

Moreover, the plebeians were ridden down heavily by debt. They were not able to stay on their farms throughout the full year, because they had to fight for the city in its frequent wars with neighboring tribes. Consequently, they were forced to go into debt. Creditors were given the right to exile debtors, or to sell them into slavery, or even to execute them.

PLEBEIANS REPRESENTED IN OFFICE OF TRIBUNE

In 494 B.C., circa, the plebeians seceded to the Sacred Mount, about three miles from the Anio River, and threatened to become a city within a city. The Senate and the patricians became uneasy because they knew they had to have the plebeians in order to fight in any war, and they were concerned that some invader might choose this particular moment to invade the city.

The Senate, accordingly, sent one of its foremost members, Menenius Agrippa, out to the Sacred Mount to plead with, and attempt to reconcile, the plebeians. To emphasize the need for cooperation between the patricians and the plebeians, he told them the famous "Fable of the Belly," a story about the interdependence of the belly and the various members of the human body. The plebeians were reconciled but only after they had gained the concession of being allowed to elect someone of their own as an official who would protect them and their property against the patricians. That official was called a tribune.

[22]

The plebeians were allowed to elect two tribunes in 494 B.C.; later, about 457 B.C., these two were increased to ten, and, in later times, they were increased to greater numbers. There were both military tribunes and civil tribunes.

Here again, we see checks and balances coming into play. Each tribune could veto the acts of the other tribune; each tribune could veto the acts of a consul; each tribune could veto and annul the *senatus consulta*: proclamations and advice of the Senate. The tribunes were declared inviolable. And the plebeians swore an oath that, if any individual interfered with a tribune, harmed him in any way, or disregarded the tribune's veto, that individual would be executed without trial. Therefore, the tribune had great power and the aura of inviolability.

Here, we see two consuls and two tribunes, the veto working back and forth, and the Senate with its three hundred members.

Then, circa 490 B.C., the Romans were at war with the Volscians, and the Romans laid siege to the town of Corioli. As the city was being besieged, a second Volscian army attacked the Romans, whereupon the besieged Volscians within the city made a sortie, and pressed the Romans from both sides. When a young Roman named Gnaeus Marcius saw that the gates were left open and that the Volscians had sallied forth from the city, he ran into the city and set the houses on fire. Amid this great confusion, the Volscians fled. The Romans prevailed, and Marcius was given the surname of Coriolanus.

Coriolanus subsequently was encouraged to run for the office of consul, but he was defeated because he made the kind of speeches that were not likely to gain the support of the electorate. In other words, he told the truth. He gave the people the facts. He was not a demagog. As a result, the people ran him out of the city. He was exiled, and he went over to the Volscians. His host there was Tullus Attius, the leader of the Volscians. In 490 B.C., Coriolanus led the Volscians, attacked the city of Rome, and camped within five miles of it.

When the Senate sent out ambassadors, leading senators who attempted to prevail upon Coriolanus to lift the siege, they were turned away.

Finally, the women of the city prevailed upon the wife and the mother of Coriolanus to go to him with his two little

[ 23 ]

sons and see if they could prevail upon him to lift the siege. The mother and wife, in the company of other women, went to the camp of Coriolanus and were introduced into his presence weeping and praying that he would lift the siege.

The historians Dionysius of Halicarnassus and Titus Livius name the mother of Coriolanus as Veturia and the wife as Volumnia, but Plutarch and Shakespeare give the mother the name of Volumnia and the wife the name of Vergilia. Livius and Dionysius give the name of the Volscian leader as Tullus Attius, whereas Shakespeare and Plutarch call the Volscian leader Tullus Aufidius. In any event, the women went outside the city walls to the camp of Coriolanus, he lifted the siege and returned to live with the Volscians.

## DICTATOR

In 458 B.C., the Romans were being hard pressed by the tribes from the east, the Aequians, and the Aequians were gaining the upper hand. A Roman general by the name of Minucius and his army had been surrounded by the Aequians for three days. The Roman Senate decided to call upon Lucius Quinctius Cincinnatus to take up the fight against the Aequians. Cincinnatus was plowing on his small three-acre farm on the west side of the Tiber, according to Livius, "just opposite the spot where the shipyards are today." The delegation from the Senate came out to the field where Cincinnatus was working with the plow. He asked them why they were there. They stated the danger from the Aequians and told him he had been selected as dictator; he was to put on his toga and rid the Romans of this threat. Whereupon, he wiped the sweat from his face and told his wife Racilia that his fields "would not be sown this year" and that they would be "in great danger of not having enough to live on." He left the farm, defeated the Aequians, laid down the dictatorship after a period of only sixteen days, and returned to his little farm and his oxen and plow.

Here we see the creation of another office, the dictatorship. A dictator could only serve for six months, or to the end of the crisis for which he was selected, whichever was the lesser. That was the utmost length of the term which a dictator could serve, but he had supreme Imperium over all other

[24]

magistrates. He had twenty-four lictors, as I have indicated. But Cincinnatus demonstrated that rare quality of not wanting to rule. He was a model of old-fashioned simplicity and ability, honesty and integrity. So, he laid down the office after only sixteen days.

By now, we have seen the office of senator, the office of consul, the office of tribune, and the office of dictator. A dictator had complete command over everything and everybody. He could command that no business be transacted, and he could raise an army, execute the laws, and put people to death.

### THE LAW OF THE TWELVE TABLES

The plebeians, meanwhile, kept agitating to have the same rights and to be governed by the same laws as the patricians were governed by. The tribunes finally prevailed upon the Senate to send a delegation to Greece to study the laws of Solon. About 454 B.C., a commission went to Greece and returned after studying the laws of Solon. In 451, ten individuals were selected and vested with all authority, all power, even over the consuls, and were given one year in which to promulgate the laws so that the plebeians would have the same knowledge of the laws and legal procedures as previously only the patricians had. The plebeians had been at a great disadvantage as a result.

The ten magistrates—decemvirs—met and over the course of a year promulgated ten tables of law. But there was still some work that remained to be done. Accordingly, the decemvirs assumed this authority for one additional year, and, during that year, two additional tables of law were produced, mainly by Lucius Valerius Potitus and Marcus Horatius Barbatus, who were members of the Roman Senate.

These were the Twelve Tables of Law, established in 450 B.C. The laws were promulgated, and inscribed, some say, on bronze tablets, others say wooden tablets, which, in turn, were displayed in the Roman forum. For a long time, these were the basic governing civil and criminal laws. The Twelve Tables were destroyed by fire when Brennus and the Gauls captured Rome in 390 B.C. But the children of the Romans had been required to memorize the Law of the Twelve Tables.

[25]

The laws were reconstructed, therefore, largely, through recollection.

In 445 B.C., under the Canuleian Law, named after a Roman tribune, the patricians and plebeians were allowed to intermarry. So, again, the plebeians had gained a right that they had been seeking for a long time.

In 443 B.C., the office of censor was created. A censor was elected once every five years for a term of eighteen months. This officer took the census and assessed the property of the Romans for the purpose of taxation. He also had jurisdiction over public contracts, and awarded contracts for buildings, highways, and other public construction. The censor could enroll people into the Senate or into the Equestrian order— about which I will have more to say later—and he could purge the rolls of senators. He could remove a senator from office because of bad conduct, public or private.

In 396 B.C., a man by the name of Marcus Furius Camillus captured the Etrurian city of Veii, which had been at war with the Romans for about ten years. Camillus was able to capture the city by burrowing a tunnel underneath it and having his men come up into the central fortress in the midst of the city. Later, he was indicted by a tribune for allegedly not having made an accurate accounting of the plunder that had resulted from the capture of Veii, and was exiled.

In 390 B.C., Brennus and the Gauls captured Rome. They executed many of its citizens and were prevailed upon to lift the siege only upon the promise of delivery by the Romans of one thousand pounds of gold, several hundred pounds of silver, and several hundred pounds of pepper, together with robes and other valuable cloth.

Camillus was requested by the Senate to come back to the city as dictator. He came back and found the Gallic chieftain and the Romans dickering over the gold. Whereupon, Camillus commanded his army to put down their baggage and prepare to fight. He said to the Romans: "It is your duty to restore your country not by gold but by the sword." He defeated the Gauls and relieved the city.

The Samnite wars took place over the period 343 B.C. to 290 B.C. Then there came the war with the Greeks who were in southern Italy, the war with Pyrrhus, King of Epirus.

[26]

I shall close my examination today of the Roman peoples. What we are observing as we go along, is a state political system that had checks and balances and a division of powers. The ancient Romans arrived at this system, not by reasoned thought but by experimentation and experience in dealing with circumstances and events as they happened, unlike Lycurgus, who, in his development of the Spartan system, did so by a process of reasoning. The Romans were not philosophers. They were practical people. Therefore, they arrived at a system through experience, trial and error, over a period of centuries, which was in some ways similar to the system developed by Lycurgus, about which I shall speak at a later time, a system which, in his case, was determined through logic and reasoning. In my next addresses to the Senate on this subject, I shall speak of Tarentum, Heraclea, Asculum, and Pyrrhus, king of Epirus.

*The Death of Remus and the Founding of Rome*

# CHAPTER 3

# The Senate Supreme

*May 18, 1993*

Mr. BYRD. Mr. President, last week I traced the history of the Roman people from the founding of the capital city of Rome in 753 B.C., through the 243 years of the monarchy to the fall of the monarchy in 510 B.C., when Tarquinius Superbus was expelled, and the founding of the republic in 509 B.C., at which time the two first Roman consuls, Lucius Junius Brutus and Tarquinius Collatinus, were chosen.

The Roman consul was the supreme civil and military magistrate of Rome under the republic. There were to be two consuls elected annually, each for a term of one year. Each consul could veto the actions of the other consul.

### PLEBEIANS PUSH FOR ADMISSION TO HIGHER MAGISTRACIES

The plebeians continued in their struggle to achieve admission to the offices and privileges of the patricians, because the monopoly of the patricians over the magistrates with Imperium deprived the plebeians of a voice in determining public policy and deprived them of the commands in the army.

The plebeian soldier shared equally with patrician soldiers the dangers in war; equality of political rights, therefore, could not forever be withheld from the plebeians. Custody of the civil and criminal law, the knowledge of civil and criminal law, of legal procedures, and the enforcement of the laws— all these were the monopoly of the patrician magistrates and priests, who naturally manipulated them to the benefit of their own classes.

One of the causes for great discontent in the later stages of this struggle was the fact that the plebeian farmers could not find the moneys with which to rent public land in order to make ends meet. The indebtedness of the plebeian land-holders was caused, in the main, by their forced absence from their lands because of military service, and also by the burden of the property tax that was levied for military purposes. Additionally, they could not acquire the capital with which to rent public land or buy additional land. Adding to this condition was the severity of the harsh laws of debt, which enabled the creditor to seize the debtor and sell him into slavery.

The first objective of the plebeians was to acquire for them-selves an officer who would act as their spokesman and who would defend them against the oppressiveness of, and exploi-tation by, the patricians. They, therefore, as I stated last week, retired to the Sacred Mount, seceded from the city, and threat-ened to become a separate city or state. They won the concession from the patricians of having an officer of their own, who could protect them against the dictates of magistrates, and that officer was the tribune.

There would be two tribunes, either of whom could veto the actions of the other tribune, the actions of any magistrate, or even the Senate, and could direct the actions of a private person.

The patricians recognized the tribunes as public officials in a sense, but not as magistrates in the strict sense of the term, because they were not elected by the whole people; they were elected only by the plebeians. The patricians also acknowledged the authority of the tribune to intervene on behalf of any person seeking aid from unjust actions by a patrician magistrate or a private person.

Legal status was given to meetings of the plebeians as long as the assembly was convened by a tribune and presided over by a tribune. But the meetings of the plebeians constitutionally were not recognized as meetings in which the actions taken would apply to the people as a whole, because the meetings were convened by a tribune and only the plebeians were sum-moned thereto by the tribune. As a consequence, the actions of such assemblies did not constitute actions by the whole people.

[ 30 ]

The plebeian assembly took place in the Roman Forum. It was not a comitia but, rather, a concilium, because only plebeians had been summoned. It was called the Concilium Plebis—a concilium meaning a meeting not of the whole people but of only a part of the people. The resolutions that were adopted in the Concilium Plebis—a meeting of the plebeians—were called plebiscites, and were binding only on the plebeians. A plebiscite was not recognized as a law that applied to the whole people, because it was not created by a body that was representative of the whole people. For the plebiscite to be valid for the whole people, it had to be ratified by the Roman Senate.

Last week, we noted the development of the following magistracies after the fall of the monarchy and the establishment of the republic: the consul, the dictator, and the censor. There was also created a magistracy referred to as the aedileship. The aedile originated as a subordinate officer of the plebeians. He was to act as an assistant to the tribunes in the oversight of the archives, the management of the prison, and the supervision of public buildings. There being two tribunes, there were two aediles.

In time, the patricians also elected two such officers and, therefore, there were four aediles. The aediles had care over the streets of Rome, over the water supply, over the market, and, especially, supervision over weights and measures. They also had responsibility for the regulation of traffic and for the conduct of the public games. In the later republic, as the wealth of the city grew and as political rivalries increased, the conduct of the public games became more and more important, and gave an opportunity to the aediles to make themselves popular and gain votes. Therefore, the aedility became a stepping stone politically.

The lowest of the regular magistracies was the quaestorship. In the beginning of the republic, the consuls appointed two financial quaestors, one quaestor to serve each consul. As time went on, the Romans increased the number of quaestors to four, and they were elected by the Tribal Assembly. Two were to serve as the state treasurers. They had immediate but limited control over the aerarium, which was the state treasury located in the Temple of Saturn below the capitol. They were to be supervised, however, by the Senate, which had full and absolute control over the aerarium. The other two quaestors were assistants to the consuls, whom they accompanied to war, where they served as quartermasters in charge of supplies and the payment of the troops.

Another magistrate was created, the office of praetor. The praetor was one of the higher magistrates. He possessed the Imperium—meaning the absolute authority to command the armies, the authority to interpret the laws and to execute the laws, the authority to inflict the death penalty.

The praetor was not allowed to leave Rome more than ten days at one time. He had the special responsibility of administering justice in the city. During the absence of both consuls from the city—if they were in the field with the legions— the praetor could convene the Senate or the Assembly, and he had the responsibility for the defense of Rome.

So, now we have the consul, the dictator, the censor, the tribune, the aedile, the quaestor, and the praetor.

The plebeians would not rest content, however, with the tribunate and the aedileship, and they, therefore, continued to press for admission to the other offices. It was not until 367 B.C. that the Licinian plebiscite required that, of the two consuls elected annually, one had to be a plebeian. But this was an enactment that was violated by the Comitia Centuriata over the next twenty-five years, and it was not until 342 B.C., under a stricter formulation of the measure, that we begin to see plebeians elected on a regular basis, one annually of the two consuls.

Of course, once the plebeians gained admission to the consulship they could no longer be barred from the other higher magistracies, such as the dictatorship or the censorship. And as it had long been the custom that ex-consuls, and later ex-praetors, were to be enrolled in the Senate's membership, the attainment of these higher magistracies meant an ever-increasing representation in the Senate by the plebeians. Therefore, we now see the plebeians becoming more and more represented by their own class in the Senate.

Now, what about the other assembly or assemblies under the republic? Was there to be only a Senate? No. The comitia

[ 32 ]

was an assembly of the Roman people summoned by a magistrate.

The earliest comitia was the assembly of the curiae. The curia was the smallest division of the Roman people. In the era of the kings, the monarch could call upon the Comitia Curiata for advice. This was an assembly of thirty curiae, ten for each of the Romulian tribes. Originally, there were three tribes. Later, urban tribes were created, and additional rustic tribes were added. The number of tribes finally reached thirty-five in the year 241 B.C. This number was never exceeded. The sixteen oldest rustic tribes bore patrician names.

Early, following the fall of the monarchy, the Comitia Centuriata came to be substituted for the Comitia Curiata. The Comitia Centuriata was made up of centuries of soldiers, a century being one hundred soldiers.

The old Comitia Curiata confirmed the appointments of magistrates. It witnessed adoptions and the writings of wills. It also witnessed the installation of priests, on which occasions the pontifex maximus would preside over the assembly.

The Comitia Centuriata came into being in the earlier years of the republic, and progressively supplanted the Comitia Curiata. The Comitia Centuriata elected the magistrates with Imperium, as well as the censor, and declared war or peace, enacted laws, and acted as judges in some capital cases.

In 287 B.C., the Hortensian Law gave greater legislative authority to the Tribal Assembly than was accorded to the Comitia Centuriata.

So, now we have witnessed, in the age of the kings, the assembly of the curiae—the Comitia Curiata—and, shortly after the fall of the monarchy, the establishment of the assembly of centuries, the Comitia Centuriata. We have also seen the development of the Concilium Plebis.

Now we see the most powerful of all the assemblies, the Comitia Tributa—the Tribal Assembly.

### SENATORIAL PREROGATIVES

In all of these, however, the actions of the assemblies were only valid if the Senate gave its approval. The Senate could exercise a veto over the actions of any of the assemblies.

[33]

We, therefore, see that the Senate remained supreme. The making of alliances and treaties, the formulation and execution of foreign policy, the waging of war, the control of the public treasury, the government of the colonies and the provinces, the management and distribution of public lands, the power over the purse—all of these were the exclusive functions of the Senate, and they gave it enormous power. The Senate also rendered judgment in such crimes as assassination, treason, and conspiracy.

The Senate met from dawn until sunset. It met in Rome, or within a mile of the city, in a place that was public and consecrated. It was summoned by a magistrate with Imperium, or, later, by a tribune. Upon the convening of the Senate, the magistrate made his report or presented the subject for discussion. After this was done, each senator was asked for his opinion in the order of rank. The senior patrician—the *Princeps Senatus*—was given precedence.

And, in time, as the Senate came to be made up of ex-magistrates, the highest of the ex-magistrates in the Senate would be called upon for his opinion; then the next highest, and then the next highest—the ex-censors, ex-consuls, ex-praetors, ex-aediles, and so on. After they had given their opinions, the vote was taken on each of the opinions by division. Senators in favor would go to one wall and be counted; senators in opposition would go to another wall and be counted. There were also other methods of division, just as there are several ways of taking a division here in the U.S. Senate.

There was absolute freedom of speech in the Roman Senate until the time of Augustus. He placed a limit on Senate speeches. But under the republic, freedom of speech was assured.

Senators, by custom, were not allowed to engage in banking or in public contracts, and they could not own a ship with carrying capacity sufficient to engage in foreign commerce. They were predominately a landlord class. They wore the *latus clavus*—a broad, purple, vertical stripe, either stitched onto, or woven into, the Roman tunic. They also wore the white toga, especially on formal occasions. They wore a special shoe, a red sandal, and it was fastened by straps that went around and up the leg.

[34]

Roman senators were given special seats at religious ceremonies, at the theater, and at other public entertainments. They were not allowed to leave Italy without permission of the Senate. This reminds us of rule VI of the standing rules of the U.S. Senate, by which, senators are supposed to get permission of the Senate for leave of absence.

How were the senators appointed? In the era of the kings, they were appointed by the king. When the monarchy came to an end in 510 B.C., and the republic was established in 509, the two first consuls were elected by the Comitia Curiata, and the consuls then appointed senators. In those early days, heredity, wealth, and being a member of a distinguished patrician family were factors that guided the selection of senators.

The censors, much later, enrolled members into the Senate. It was the plebiscite of Ovinius, a tribune, that formulated regulations by which senators were to be enrolled in that body. Following the Ovinian plebiscite, the censors were expected to abide by the law, which required, in the enrollment of senators, that precedence be given to all worthy ex-magistrates. The Senate, therefore, became, largely, a body of ex-magistrates—men who had served as consuls, praetors, and other magistracies; men who had held command of the armies. Consuls commanded legions; praetors also had authority to command the legions. Hence, here was an experienced body of generals and former high administrative officials. Consequently, the Senate was the gathering of the wisest, the most experienced men in public life.

### The Roman Character

Now, let us take just a moment to talk about the Roman family. The capital stone, the cornerstone of the Roman social structure was the family. The father had complete authority over everyone in the family. It was there that the sons and daughters were taught discipline and respect for authority. They were taught to reverence, and to sacrifice to, the gods. They were taught to venerate their ancestors. Such discipline and respect for authority were carried over by the Roman into his public relations, and it aroused in him a sense of duty to foster the interests of the state. This was a basic quality of the Roman character. For the Romans, the highest virtue was loyalty—loyalty to one's oath, to parents and family, to the gods, and to the state. Dutifulness in religion and respect for authority were engrained from the earliest childhood years. Loyalty to the state was overriding, and the ancient Roman was prepared, if necessary, to make the supreme sacrifice of life itself for the state. One cannot doubt, therefore, the importance of these basic values in Roman life, as passing generations of Romans would look back with awe and admiration to their ancestors of the early and middle republic to find examples of statesmanship and heroism worthy of emulation.

The sense of duty ran deep. A Roman who was suited for, and inclined toward, public service felt that it was his responsibility to serve the state, in public office, certainly in public life, or in the military. This was his duty.

The Romans believed in the principle that was enthusiastically enunciated and maintained by Cicero: that it was the civic duty of the citizen to serve in public office and in public life.

Since public office and public service were never regarded as a profession, no remuneration was given to Roman magistrates. Senators served only for the honor of serving the state, and without pay. They had seats for life unless they were guilty of grave misconduct. The only remuneration for Roman magistrates was for journeys or special celebrations or for military commands and expenses, and so forth. It was one's duty to serve the Roman state. Senators believed that service in that body was the highest honor, and that attendance at sessions of the Senate was an integral part of that service.

This high sense of duty emerged from a dialogue between the Emperor Vespasian and the Senator Helvidius Priscus, as written by Epictetus. When the Emperor Vespasian sent word to Helvidius not to attend a meeting of the Senate, Helvidius answered: "It is in your power not to allow me to be a member of the Senate, but as long as I am one, I must attend its meetings."

Plutarch tells us that the same high sense of duty was demonstrated by Marcus Porcius Cato the Younger, who lived between 95 and 46 B.C.:

> There was no meeting of the Senate which he did not attend, in order to keep a watchful eye upon all partial remissions

of fines and duties and all unreasonable grants. . . . Whenever the Senate was summoned to meet he was the first to give his attendance and the last to withdraw. . . . He thought that a good citizen ought to be as solicitous about the public, as a bee is about her hive.

Hence, Mr. President, we have witnessed the stern self-discipline, the respect for authority, the high sense of duty, the old Roman virtues that formed the sterling Roman character. We have also noted the development over time of various magistracies that were held by men who served not to fulfill pecuniary ambitions, but, instead, by men who had an overweening ambition to give themselves to the service of the Roman state.

We have discussed the consuls and the praetors, who had the Imperium—the authority to command armies, to execute the laws, to execute soldiers under their command, or to impose the sentence of death on people within the city of Rome, to execute without trial. At a later point, this power was taken away from the consuls and they could no longer execute individuals within the city of Rome or within one mile of the city without trial.

We have again seen a separation of powers—the quaestors who had supervision over issuance of payments to soldiers and who also had supervision over the public treasury, the aerarium in Rome, always, however, under the final and absolute control of the Senate. The Senate had the complete power over the purse. The consuls could issue their vouchers in the field, but the Senate, before those vouchers could be paid, had to approve the payments.

These were checks and balances—one consul being able to veto the acts of the other consul, one tribune being able to veto the acts of other tribunes or consuls or other higher magistrates with the exception of the dictator. We have also followed the creation of the various assemblies, or comitias, and we have observed that their actions could be vetoed by the Senate— another check and balance.

In the Roman republic, from its earliest days, through the early republic and the middle republic, the Senate was supreme.

[ 37 ]

Little wonder that the average Roman was inspired as he looked back upon the examples of statesmen and generals of earlier times, inspired to give of his best, inspired to serve his country. Little wonder that the ancient Romans acquired control over the surrounding tribes and stretched their supremacy from the Gallic north throughout the entire Italian peninsula. Little wonder that this small, fledgling city that was founded on the river Tiber, came to be the greatest city of antiquity and to rule over the greatest empire of antiquity. Mr. President, I yield the floor.

*There is a wheel on which the affairs of men revolve, and its movement forbids the same man to be always fortunate.*

Croesus

தஓஜ

*History, by apprising [men] of the past, will enable them to judge of the future.*

Thomas Jefferson

தஓஜ

*We may gather out of history a policy no less wise than eternal; by the comparison and application of other men's forepassed miseries with our own like errors and ill deservings.*

Sir Walter Raleigh

தஓஜ

*The use of history is to give value to the present hour and its duty.*

Ralph Waldo Emerson

தஓஜ

*People will not look forward to posterity who never look backward to their ancestors.*

Edmund Burke

*Manlius Torquatus Condemns His Son to Death*

# CHAPTER 4

# Roman Unification of the Italian Peninsula

*May 25, 1993*

Mr. BYRD. Madam President, today I continue in my series of speeches concerning the line-item veto, with particular emphasis on the history of the Romans.

Now, why am I doing this? These speeches do not make any headlines. My staff does not rush out with press releases. The speeches are not expected to make news.

### To Enhance Public Understanding

I hope by these speeches to enhance the understanding and the appreciation of all those who will listen—members of the Senate, members of the House, representatives of the press, and the public in general. I hope to enhance their understanding of the importance of maintaining a legislative branch that is free of domination from an all-powerful executive, and of the critical role that the power over the purse plays in the constitutional mechanism of separation of powers and checks and balances handed down to us by the constitutional framers in Philadelphia in the year 1787.

Why history? Because many, if not most, of the Framers were conversant with Roman history and with the history of England. They were also familiar with the political philosophy of Montesquieu, whose political theory of checks and balances and separation of powers influenced them in their writing of the Constitution. Montesquieu was also influenced in his political philosophy by the history of the Romans, by contemporary English institutions, and by English history.

[ 41 ]

And so, Madam President, I proceed, then, with another in my series of speeches on the history of the Romans.

### ADDITIONAL MAGISTRACIES

In 509 B.C., the Romans switched from a king as the executive to the election of two consuls as dual executives, with equal powers; both to be elected at the same time, each to be elected for a one-year term, and each having a veto over the other consul's actions. To avoid an overuse of the veto, the two consuls alternated from month to month in taking charge of the administration when both were in the city. And when both were in the field, they alternated from day to day in holding the chief command of the Roman legions. This duality and collegiality represented by two consuls, constituted the Roman answer to any possible threat of a return to monarchical rule.

In addition to the two consuls, we noted last week the development of various other magistracies. Today, I would like to add three: The interrex, the master of the horse, and the proconsul.

The interrex was an individual appointed by the Senate upon the death of a king, with provisional authority to rule until another king was chosen. Later, during the republic, an interrex was appointed when both consuls died or resigned—their seats being vacant. And he was to rule with the Imperium, the authority of a consul. He was to have twelve lictors, who would escort him. The interrex had to be a patrician and he had to be a senator. His appointment lasted for only a few days.

The master of the horse was nominated by a dictator to serve as the dictator's subordinate and commander of cavalry. He could take the place of the dictator in the field or in Rome. The Imperium of the master of the horse was a derivative of the dictator's Imperium, and the master of the horse ended his commission when the dictator laid down his office. Under the Roman constitution, the dictator could only serve a maximum of six months or until his task was done, whichever was the lesser.

The Roman people created the office of proconsul in 327 B.C., as Quintus Publilius Philo (author of the publilian laws), a consul, was besieging the city of Naples and was about to capture it. Just then, his one-year term of office expired. What was to be done? He no longer had the authority to command the armies. The Roman people voted his continuing Imperium, but for no more than a year, or for such time as was needed to complete his task, whichever was the lesser. Therefore, his command of the army, his Imperium, his office of consul, was continued temporarily into the next year, 326 B.C. It meant that, as proconsul, Publilius was to continue to act as consul for a limited time after his regular term of office as consul had expired.

### THE SENATE

From the beginning of the era of the kings, there was an assembly of the people. The first assembly was the comitia, meaning "assembly"—the Comitia Curiata, made up of the curiae. There then followed the Comitia Centuriata, which was an assembly of centuries; then, the Concilium Plebis, or council of the plebeians; then, the Comitia Tributa, the tribal assembly. And, in the case of each of these assemblies, the convening of the assembly had to be by a magistrate. The assembly could only vote up or down on the subject matter presented by the presiding magistrate. The assembly could not amend the proposal. The Senate could veto the actions of the assembly. In order, therefore, for the actions of the people's assembly to become law, the actions had to have the ratification or approval of the Senate. The Senate was supreme.

In the fourth century, the plebiscite of Ovinius, a Roman tribune, was enacted. It presented a formulation of regulations by which individuals were to be enrolled into the Senate as members thereof. The plebiscite gave preference to ex-magistrates. So, by law, the censors, who enrolled members into the Senate, were required to give preference to worthy ex-magistrates.

What did this mean? This meant that the exercise of excessive personal or factional influence over the composition of the Senate was curbed. It also meant that the guarantee of a future seat for life in the Senate was an incentive to every magistrate to do his best during his tenure of office, to act honorably and to serve effectively so that he would be considered an

[43]

individual worthy, when his term of office ended, of enrollment as a member of the Senate. Moreover, it meant that the Senate, albeit indirectly, was popularly elected, because it was made up of ex-magistrates who had had to stand for election before entering upon their various offices—the consuls, the censors, the praetors, the quaestors, and so forth. Thus, the Senate, for the most part, being a body of ex-magistrates, was a gathering of the wisest men in Rome—men who had held high administrative positions in the government, or had commanded armies in the field, or both, before entering the Senate.

The Senate held the power over the purse. It was supreme in financial matters. It regulated the coinage, it determined the rate of tribute, it supervised the revenues and the expenditures, it controlled the aerarium.

The aerarium was the state treasury, located in the Temple of Saturn below the capitol, and was in the care of two quaestors. In the aerarium were the silver and gold ingots, the bronze lumps and bars, and, after 269 B.C., the Roman coins that were made of silver and bronze. Some of the other tribes had proceeded with the manufacture of coins before the Romans did. Also in the aerarium were the papers, the documents of state. It was the receptacle of the *senatus consulta*. What was a *senatus consultum*? A *senatus consultum* was the advice of the Senate to a magistrate. In republican times, it did not have legislative force, but, de facto, it was binding.

I said last week that the Roman Senate met from dawn until sunset. The *senatus consultum* was drafted after the day's session of the Senate, in the presence of the presiding magistrate and in the presence of witnesses, included among whom was the proposer or author of the *senatus consultum*.

The *senatus consultum* contained the name of the presiding magistrate, the date, the place of assembly, and the terms or substance of the *senatus consultum*. It indicated the number of senators who were present when the *senatus consultum* was approved. It also gave the names of witnesses to the drafting of the *senatus consultum*, and it included the capital letter "C," indicating that the Senate had given its approval. The texts of the *senatus consulta* were deposited in the aerarium.

Plutarch writes that before the consulate of Marcus Tullius Cicero, who lived between 106 B.C. and 43 B.C., there were

[44]

no shorthand writers. Cicero had recruited a number of the swiftest writers, and he taught them the art of abbreviating words by characters. He placed them in various parts of the Senate house. The records were filed in the aerarium.

## SAMNITE WARS, 343–290 B.C.

Madam President, from the very earliest times, the Romans seemed to be incessantly involved in fighting battles with neighboring tribes. From time to time, the Romans would lose a battle, but they always won the war.

One such battle was the battle of Caudine Forks in 321 B.C. It took place during the Samnite wars. Gaius Pontius was the general leading the Samnites on this occasion. The two Roman consuls were Titus Venturius Calvinus and Spurius Postumius. These two Roman consuls and their armies were on their way to Luceria. There were two routes by which they could go, but the Samnite general lured them into choosing the shorter, and the more dangerous, of the two routes. The route that they chose led through two gorges—steep, wooded, and narrow. Between the two gorges, there was a wide, grassy plain. The road ran through the center of this valley.

The Romans passed through the first gorge and emerged into the valley. As they proceeded to the second pass, they found it blocked by a barrier of large rocks and fallen trees. At the head of the pass, they noticed some armed men, and it was apparent that they had fallen into a trap. They quickly retreated to the other gorge from which they had entered into the valley, but they found it, by then, likewise barricaded with rocks and controlled by armed Samnites. Every effort to extricate themselves was in vain. Finally, their supplies ran out, and they were driven to attempt to make a reasonable, honorable peace.

The two consuls consulted with Pontius, the enemy general, who stated that he was prepared to make a treaty if the Romans would vacate Samnite territory. The two consuls insisted that they were not authorized to make a treaty without the approval of the Roman people. The Romans were then ordered to leave immediately and to lay down their arms. The two consuls were ordered to dismiss their lictors and to remove their cloaks, their general's cloaks. The two generals were then forced to

[45]

walk under the yoke. The yoke was two spears erected vertically a few feet apart, with a third spear across the two upright spears. The legions, made up of twenty thousand Romans, were also forced to march under the yoke. They had to bend to go beneath the yoke. And they were stripped of every bit of clothing, except for a single garment. They were forced, therefore, to walk half-naked, while on each side, the enemy soldiers were armed and stood there cursing and taunting the Roman legions as they marched beneath the yoke.

### TARENTINE CAMPAIGNS

The expressions on the faces of the Romans, imaginably, were expressions of humiliation and embarrassment, the expressions of captives. They entered the city of Rome far into the night and stole away, each to his own house. The next day, not one of them ventured forth into the Forum or into the public streets. It was a terrible defeat for the Romans. But, as Montesquieu said, the Romans "never sought peace except as victors. They always increased their demands in proportion to their defeats." The more disastrous a defeat, the more the stakes went up, the more the Romans increased the ante, the more they increased their demands on the enemy. They were an indomitable people.

The Samnite wars, which continued sporadically from 343 B.C. to 290 B.C., ended with the Romans victorious. It was apparent then that the Romans, having conquered the Samnites—who were an ancient people in southern Italy, living in the Apennines—intended to extend their sway throughout the whole peninsula.

The rich Greek city of Tarentum resented the penetration of the Romans into southern Italy. The Romans had established a garrison at Thurium, not far from Tarentum, and the Romans enhanced that garrison by providing a squadron of ten galleys to cruise in the Gulf of Tarentum. One day, the Tarentines saw these galleys at the entrance of the port in the Gulf of Tarentum. The Tarentines immediately manned their own vessels, went out and attacked the Roman squadron, destroyed four of the galleys, took one, and butchered the crew. Emboldened by this seemingly easy success, they then drove out the garrison from Thurium and plundered the city.

[46]

Shortly thereafter, a Roman ambassador, Lucius Postumius Megellus, appeared and demanded reparations. He had been sent by the Senate. The Tarentines gave him an audience in the theater, and he used such Greek as he could command. He did not do very well with the language. Each time he placed the wrong accent on a word, the Tarentines would burst out in a laugh. And when he remonstrated, they laughed all the more. They called him a barbarian and, at last, hissed him off the stage. As the grave Roman senator retired, a Tarentine, who, by his constant drunkenness, had been nick-named the "Pint-Pot," came up to Megellus with gestures of the grossest indecency and bespattered the senatorial gown with filth. Megellus turned to the multitude and held up the bespattered gown, as though appealing to a universal law of nations. At this sight, the Tarentines burst out in even greater laughter. They set up such a loud laugh as shook the theater. Megellus paused. "Men of Tarentum," he said, "laugh. Laugh now. It will take not a little blood to wash this gown."

The Romans then advanced on Tarentum, whereupon the Tarentines invited Pyrrhus, a Greek general, to descend upon Italy. Pyrrhus was king of Epirus and was the most able of all of those who claimed to be the heirs of Alexander. His words, when he saw the encampment of Romans, were full of meaning: "These barbarians have nothing barbarous in their military arrangements." He sought to negotiate with the Romans. He proposed that if they would leave Tarentum and the other Greek cities free, and if they would restore to the Samnites, the Apulians, the Lucanians, and the Bruttiums, the cities and the lands which the Romans had taken from them, he then would offer to enter into an alliance with the Romans.

But the Romans repelled every offer. Pyrrhus had brought with him 25,000 men, well trained in the Macedonian battle formation. He had also brought twenty elephants. This is the first occasion on which elephants had been seen on the Roman peninsula. Alexander the Great had encountered elephants in his battles with Darius III at Issus in 333 B.C., and at the battle of Arbela, sometimes referred to as the battle of Gaugamela, in 331 B.C.

[47]

The Romans were not prepared for the onset of the elephants and they lost the battle of Heraclea. Pyrrhus won, but at great cost.

Pyrrhus, in crossing the Adriatic, had counted on an easy war. Instead, he had met with the most redoubtable of adversaries. He renewed his peace proposal to the Romans. He offered again the same proposal, but this time he added a provision that he would free all Roman prisoners without ransom. Cineas, the philosopher, was charged by Pyrrhus to submit the proposals to Rome. Cineas spoke before the Roman Senate. He had brought with him bribes for Roman senators, and rich robes for senators' wives. But he found no takers. He found no one venal, but he made an eloquent speech to the Roman Senate. Pyrrhus had once said that the eloquence of Cineas had gained for him, Pyrrhus, more cities than had been gained by arms. Cineas almost persuaded the Roman Senate to accept the peace proposals by Pyrrhus.

Appius Claudius Caecus was a renowned Roman who has been compared to the aristocratic founders of Athenian democracy. When he was censor in 312 B.C., he enrolled in the Senate several persons of low birth, plebeians, and the sons of freedmen. He did this in order to get their votes, their support for his plan to build a highway, the Via Appia, into southern Italy, and his plan to construct the first aqueduct, the Aquae Appia. The cardinal feature in the policy of Appius Claudius Caecus was to enlarge Roman control over the entire Italian peninsula.

When Caecus heard that the members of the Senate were about to be convinced by the silver-tongued Cineas, he had his servants carry him to the Senate house, whereupon his sons and sons-in-law led him into the Senate. He was old. He was blind. When Caecus—who had been censor, consul, praetor, interrex, and dictator—entered the Senate, he was met with a silence of respect.

He said, as related by Plutarch:

> Hitherto, I have regarded my blindness as a misfortune. But today, Romans, I wish I were as deaf as I am blind. For then, I would not have heard the reports of your shameful counsels and decrees, so ruinous to the glory of Rome. You tremble at the name of Pyrrhus. Do not expect that, to

[48]

enter into an alliance with him, you will rid yourselves of him. That step will only open a door to many invaders. For who is there who will not despise you and think you an easy conquest if Pyrrhus not only escapes unpunished for his insolence, but also gains the Tarentines and Samnites as a reward for insulting the Romans? Tell Pyrrhus to leave Italy. Then we will talk with him.

When Caecus concluded his speech, the senators voted unanimously to continue the war. They told Cineas that if Pyrrhus continued to stay in Italy, he would be pursued with force, even though he should have defeated a thousand Laevinuses— Laevinus having been the Roman consul who was defeated at Heraclea. The senators ordered Cineas to leave town that day, after they had levied two additional Roman legions right before his eyes.

Cineas was impressed. The sight of this great city, its austere manners, and its patriotic zeal struck Cineas with admiration. And when he had heard the deliberations of the Senate and observed its men, he reported to Pyrrhus that here was no mere gathering of venal politicians, no haphazard council of mediocre minds, but, in dignity and statesmanship, veritably "an assemblage of kings." Cineas told Pyrrhus that it would be a mistake for Pyrrhus to continue in this war with the Romans, because they were in such great numbers, they could create new legions so fast that Pyrrhus would find himself engaged in a war with the Lernaean hydra, which was a serpent or monster with nine heads that lived in the marshes near Lerna. According to legend, each time Hercules had cut off one head, two more appeared, unless the wounds were cauterized.

Pyrrhus fought a second battle at Asculum with the Romans in 279 B.C. The Romans were defeated again, with great losses on both sides. At the conclusion of the battle, he exclaimed, "Such another victory, and we are undone." But in 275 B.C., the Romans defeated Pyrrhus at Beneventum, and he returned to Epirus with only a third of his expeditionary force. In 272 B.C., Tarentum fell, conquered by the Romans. With its fall, the Romans, who had founded the little fledgling city on the banks of the Tiber five hundred years before, now controlled the entire peninsula from the Po valley in the north to the

[49]

Ionian Sea in the south, from the Tyrrhenian Sea on the west to the Adriatic on the east.

MANLIAN DISCIPLINE

What was the secret of their success? Well, of course, there were several secrets of their success, one of which was their superior military system. The consuls commanded the armies in the field. The consuls may not have been always great, or even good, generals, but they were always soldiers of experience, because it was a requirement of a candidate for office in Rome during the republic that he had to have a record of at least ten military campaigns. And the subordinates of the consuls, the military tribunes, were also veterans, because they, too, had to experience five or ten campaigns. The consular Imperium gave to its holder absolute power over the soldier in the field, and the penalty of neglect of duty, cowardice, or disobedience was death.

The main factor in the military success of the Romans was the iron discipline—the iron discipline and respect for authority that the Romans had learned first at the hearth in the home.

There is one example of Roman discipline I shall mention here that will suffice. In 340 B.C., the Roman armies were fighting the Volscians, Campanians, and Latins. The Roman armies were encamped near the city of Capua in southern Italy. The two Roman consuls were Titus Manlius Imperiosus Torquatus and Decius. The Roman consuls felt that, if there ever were a time when military discipline was vitally important, it was on this occasion, because they were fighting against people who had the same language, customs, weapons, and the same battle tactics as their own. Many times, the Romans— the common soldiers, the centurions, the tribunes—had mingled and fraternized together in the same companies with the enemy. Therefore, the two consuls felt that, in order to avoid confusion that might end in a terribly disastrous error, they should pronounce an edict that no Roman should leave his rank to attack the enemy until commanded or ordered to do so by the Roman consuls.

The edict was issued. The soldiers then went out upon patrols, reconnoitering the territory, and the leader of one of these Roman patrols was Titus Manlius, the son of Titus Manlius

[50]

Imperiosus Torquatus, the consul. Young Manlius and his squadron came near the enemy. The commander of the cavalry of the enemy was named Geminus Maecius. As he saw the Roman patrol approaching, he recognized the leader of the patrol as the son of the Roman consul. He challenged Titus Manlius to fight. The other soldiers stood back, and Titus Manlius, in the anger of the moment, forgot the edict of the consuls and plunged forth to do battle. The two horses and their riders rushed toward one another. Titus Manlius charged with such force that he drove his spear into the mouth of Geminus Maecius, and it emerged between his ribs. Titus Manlius then removed the spoils of the enemy and carried them back to the tent of his father, the Roman consul. When he told his father what had happened, his father turned his back on his son and ordered that the trumpet be sounded for an assembly.

When the assembly had gathered, the father then turned to his son and said:

> You, Titus Manlius, have respected neither the edict of the consuls nor the authority of your father. You have undermined the military discipline upon which Roman power has always depended. Because of this, it is better that we be punished for our sins than that the republic suffer to atone for our transgressions. I am affected both by the inborn love of a father and by these tokens of your courage. But the orders of the consuls must either be confirmed by your death or be forever nullified by your immunity. Go, lictor, bind him to the stake!

This was the "Manlian discipline" that was so often referred to by posterity. It was a harsh discipline, but it taught Roman soldiers to be obedient to the orders of their commanders. And it was said that Roman soldiers feared their commanders more than they feared the enemy, because they knew what the penalty would be for disobedience, for cowardice, or for neglect of duty.

### SUMMING UP

Now, with the unification of all Italy we have brought the Romans to the point where they were becoming increasingly involved in international affairs. But, for the moment, let us recapitulate.

We have seen a Roman constitutional system develop through chance, experience, trial and error—a Roman system of checks and balances—the veto of each consul as against the acts of the other, the veto of each plebeian tribune as against the acts of the other or the acts of the consuls. We have noted the origin and development of the assemblies of the people. We have also seen that their legislative actions could not become law without the approval of the Senate—another check and balance.

We have observed the Senate as an institution that existed from the beginning, from the very first king, the legendary Romulus, who appointed one hundred of the wisest men to the Senate. We saw its membership increase by one hundred under Tarquinius Priscus, and we saw the membership increase by an additional one hundred under the first Roman consul, Lucius Junius Brutus, in 509 B.C.

We saw the Senate supreme. We have noted that it had absolute control over the purse. We have noted that it was free from the domination of any consul, free from domination by the executive.

We have witnessed the separation of powers in the Roman system—the consuls, the tribunes, the quaestors, the praetors, the aediles, the interrex, the proconsuls, the master of the horse, and so on—some to act as judges, some to act as administrators, some to act as legislators in assemblies, others in the Roman Senate.

The Senate had control over the treasury. While the assemblies declared war or peace, it was the Senate that waged war. We have watched the Senate wage wars and emerge victorious—the wars with the Tarentines, the Samnites, the Apulians, the Lucanians, and with Pyrrhus and the Greeks.

We have seen a Senate that was made up of wise men, the wisest in the state—wisest because they were selected through the process of experience that guaranteed that there would be a body of men who had held command of the armies in the field, and others who had held high positions in government. A pillar of strength—that was the Roman Senate.

[52]

We have marvelled at the respect for authority and the imposition of discipline that began with the child in the Roman family, in the home—not only a respect for authority, but also a reverence for the gods. They were pagan gods, to be sure, but there was reverence for the gods. It was that respect for authority, that discipline, that reverence for the gods, that made the Roman character what it was and made the Romans so victorious in battle. Each Roman believed that Rome had a god-decreed destiny to be fulfilled, and each Roman believed that it was his personal duty to assist in achieving that destiny, the destiny of his country.

We can discern so many parallels in the long Roman history with our own beginnings in our own country. And as we proceed, we shall note the continuing ascendancy of the Roman state and the Roman people, and then we shall observe the beginning of the decline, a slow but fatal decline. We shall find that as long as the Roman Senate was independent of the dominance of any executive, Rome grew in strength and influence. We shall also see that when the Roman Senate declined and was dominated by an all-powerful dictator or emperor or by the Praetorian Guard, Rome also declined.

I yield the floor.

*Regulus Leaves Rome to Return to Carthage*

# CHAPTER 5

# The First and Second Punic Wars

*June 9, 1993*

Mr. BYRD. Mr. President, when I last spoke on this subject, I spoke of the provocations by the city of Tarentum which resulted in the visitation by a Roman senator, Lucius Postumius Megellus, who demanded reparations from the Tarentines for the destruction of four Roman galleys, the taking of another, and the butchering of the Roman crew. I also spoke of the insults that were heaped upon Postumius by the Tarentines, and of the drunken Philonides who stood at the exit of the theater, as Postumius was prepared to retire, and, being full of yesterday's wine, bespattered the Roman's toga with filth. This created a great deal of amusement among the Tarentines and the theater rocked with their laughter. Postumius exclaimed: "Laugh, laugh while you may, Tarentines! For long will be the time when you will weep hereafter. It will take not a little blood to wash this robe."

The Tarentines, as we noted, called in Pyrrhus, the king of Epirus, the great Greek general. We noted the battle of Heraclea in 280 B.C. and the battle of Asculum in 279 B.C., in both of which battles Pyrrhus was victorious but suffered severe losses. He was defeated at the battle of Beneventum in 275 B.C. So struck with admiration for Roman valor was Pyrrhus that he exclaimed, "How easy it were for me to win the empire of the world if I had an army of Romans, or for the Romans to win if they had me as their king."

THE CARTHAGINIAN CHALLENGE

We noted that in 272 B.C., the city of Tarentum fell, and this completed the domination of the Italian peninsula by the

Romans. With the unification of Italy, Rome entered upon a new era in her foreign relations. The city-state of Carthage at this time was the dominant power in the Mediterranean. Carthage was located on the northern coast of Africa, about where the city of Tunis is today. Carthage had been a colony of the Phoenician city of Tyre, and when the Phoenician cities in Asia Minor had passed under the control of the Babylonians in the sixth century B.C., and had been incorporated into the Persian Empire, Carthage and other Phoenician settlements severed their ties with the homeland. Carthage had been founded in the latter part of the eighth century, although in the opinion of some historians, it had been founded a century earlier, in 814 B.C., in the latter part of the ninth century. Carthage was a trading power. She was not militaristically aggressive. She depended upon trade and commerce for her prosperity. And she dominated the western Mediterranean from Sicily to Gibraltar.

Having a commercial monopoly in the western Mediterranean, it was necessary for Carthage to be a naval power, and she was the undisputed mistress of the seas from the Strait of Messina in northeast Sicily to the Strait of Gibraltar and beyond, north and south on the Atlantic coast. She possessed most of Sicily except for the town of Messina, on the northeast corner, and Syracuse in the southeast. She also possessed Sardinia, Corsica, the Balearic Islands, the other islands in the western Mediterranean, and most of Iberia—now Spain—from which she received agricultural products, silver, copper, and iron. She received tin from what is now England, and ivory and gold from the west coast of Africa.

Carthage, unlike Rome, had no organized national army. She depended upon mercenaries recruited from war-like peoples, such as the Spaniards, the Libyans, and the Gauls. This was the state which Rome now faced following her subjugation of southern Italy. This was the power which Rome would challenge in a war for dominion beyond the peninsula.

The first war between Rome and Carthage grew out of the political situation in Sicily, where a band of Campanian mercenaries had occupied the city of Messina and had become a menace to their neighbors, the Syracusans. King Hiero of Syracuse was at the point of conquering Messina when the

[56]

Campanians appealed to the Carthaginians for assistance. The Carthaginians responded by establishing a garrison in Messina. It was not long before the Campanian mercenaries, who called themselves Mamertines, realized that they had slipped out of the frying pan into the fire, because the Carthaginians showed no indications of leaving. The Campanian mercenaries, therefore, appealed to Rome to help them get rid of the Carthaginians.

FIRST PUNIC WAR, 264–241 B.C.

The Roman Senate was quick to note that the occupation of Messina by the Carthaginians would put the Carthaginians in control of the Strait of Messina, and would constitute a perpetual threat to southern Italy, and eventually to Rome itself. Therefore, the Roman Senate authorized the levy of two Roman legions, and they were dispatched to Sicily in 264 B.C. This was the beginning of the First Punic War. There were three Punic wars, so designated by Cicero. Actually, it was one war extending intermittently from 264 B.C. to 146 B.C., a total of 118 years. But the first stage of the war, referred to as the First Punic War, lasted from 264 B.C. to 241 B.C. Rome, therefore, found itself at war with Carthage in 264 B.C.

By 261 B.C., the Roman Senate realized the necessity for creating a large naval fleet which could challenge the naval supremacy of Carthage, and the Romans used as their model a Carthaginian warship which had washed ashore and been left stranded. Within a few months, the Romans had built 120 vessels, of which 100 were quinqueremes and 20 were triremes. The triremes were manned by 150 rowers, each manipulating one oar. Each quinquereme had a complement of 300 rowers and 120 fighting men. The quinquereme had huge oars, each manned by five rowers. The quinquereme was the first-class battleship of the day, quite an undertaking for the Romans, who had never before had warships, never before had a navy.

In 260 B.C., a Roman consul by the name of Gaius Duilius, commander of the Roman naval fleet, challenged a superior Carthaginian fleet off Mylae, at the northeastern tip of Sicily, and destroyed the Carthaginian fleet. It was a victory as decisive as it was surprising.

In 256 B.C., the Romans landed a consul and his consular army in Africa. His name was Marcus Atilius Regulus, and at first he was victorious over the Carthaginians. But in 255 B.C., he met with a serious disaster in connection with which he himself was taken prisoner. The Carthaginians treated their Roman prisoners with consideration, except for Regulus, whom they kept in a state of utter misery. They gave him just enough food to stay alive, and they constantly paraded a huge elephant near him so as to frighten him and allow him no peace of body or mind.

In 249 B.C., the Carthaginians decided to send envoys to Rome to propose peace, and they sent Marcus Atilius Regulus, the Roman consul, along with the envoys, believing that their object would be gained by virtue of the standing and valor of the man. The Carthaginians exacted from Regulus, before he left Carthage, an oath to return to Carthage without fail. When Regulus was brought into the Senate house, he explained to the Romans that he had been sent with the envoys to make a peace that would be pleasing to both parties, if possible; but if this was not possible, he was to try to effect an exchange of prisoners.

The Roman Senate asked Regulus for his opinion. Regulus, according to the historian Cassius Dio Cocceianus, answered:

> As a prisoner of the Carthaginians, my body is a Carthaginian chattel, but my spirit is yours. As a captive, I belong to the Carthaginians; yet, inasmuch as I met with misfortune, not from cowardice but from zeal, I am not only a Roman, but I also have your cause at heart. Not in one single respect do I think reconciliation advantageous to you.

The Roman Senate then, out of consideration for Regulus' safety, showed a disposition to free the captives; whereupon, Regulus explained his reasons for believing that the rejection of the Carthaginian proposal was in the interest of the Romans. He added: "I know that manifest destruction awaits me, for it is impossible to keep them from learning the advice I have given you. Even so, I esteem my country's advantage above my own safety." When the Roman consuls suggested that Regulus remain in Rome and not return to Carthage as a prisoner, Regulus answered, "I have sworn to them to return, and I

[58]

will not transgress my oaths, not even when they have been given to enemies." Hence, no agreement was reached with the envoys, and no exchange of prisoners was made.

When Regulus was departing in the company of the Carthaginian envoys, his wife and little children clung to him tearfully. The Senate told Regulus that they would not surrender him if he chose to stay, but, inasmuch as he was determined to keep the oath that he had given, he was sent back to Carthage, where he was tortured to death. The Carthaginians cut off his eyelids, and cast him into a specially constructed enclosure bristling with spikes, and made him face the sun. Therefore, from his suffering and sleeplessness—the spikes would not allow him to recline in any fashion—he perished. Mr. President, this is an example of a Roman who valued his oath above his life. Montesquieu said, "The Romans were the most religious people in the world when it came to an oath, which always formed the nerve of their military discipline."

Mr. President, the Constitution of the United States in Article VI requires senators, representatives, members of the state legislatures, and all executive and judicial officers, state and federal, to take an oath to support and defend the Constitution of the United States. Six times I have stood before the Senate and sworn, by that oath, to support and defend the Constitution of the United States against all enemies foreign and domestic. And many times I have stood at that desk as the president pro tempore and administered the oath to others who were entering upon the office of senator.

How serious do we regard this oath? Sometimes I wonder if we ever think of it again until the next six years have passed and we again take the oath upon being reelected to the office of senator. The Constitution provides that the power of the purse shall be vested in the Congress of the United States. We swear before God—our Maker, Creator of life and life eternal—and before man that we will support and defend that Constitution. Yet, there are those in this body who would support the shifting of that power over the purse, at least in part, to the chief executive. We ought to be serious about that oath. We ought to remember that the Constitution vests the power of the purse in the legislative branch.

Regulus was true to his oath, and we should be true to ours.

In 247 B.C., Hamilcar Barca, a new Carthaginian general, was appointed to the command in Sicily. He infused new life, new enthusiasm into the Carthaginian cause. Hamilcar was a military genius. He kept the Romans at bay for the next six years until, in 242 B.C., a Roman fleet under Lutatius Catulus destroyed a Carthaginian relief expedition at the battle of the Aegates Islands, just west of northern Sicily. It was impossible for the Carthaginians to prolong the struggle further in view of the fact that they were completely cut off in Sicily. Therefore, Carthage was forced to sue for peace, and peace was restored in 241 B.C. The result of the First Punic War was that Carthage gave up Sicily to the Romans.

Immediately following peace, a war broke out in Carthage, because the mercenaries who had been employed by the government of Carthage to fight the Romans in Sicily were not paid in accordance with the promises of the Carthaginian government. The mercenary war in Carthage lasted three years. The mercenaries were finally cruelly put down by Hamilcar Barca. During this time, when Carthage was suffering in extremis, the Roman Senate saw the opportunity to take advantage of Carthage's vulnerabilities and seized Sardinia and Corsica.

In 237 B.C., the Carthaginians dispatched a new army under the command of Hamilcar Barca to Spain, and for eight years, Hamilcar Barca, through the arts of diplomacy and also through the making of war, reduced many of the Iberian tribes to loyalty to Carthage. In 229 B.C., Hamilcar Barca died in a manner that was worthy of his great achievements, for he perished in a battle with the most warlike and powerful tribes, during which battle he showed a conspicuous and even reckless personal gallantry.

Diodorus of Sicily, the historian, writes that, on this occasion, Hamilcar, having been betrayed by an Iberian king's feigned offer of friendship and alliance, ordered those who were with him to flee. When his sons—Hannibal, aged fifteen, and Hasdrubal, aged twelve—clung to him and desired to share his death, he drove them off with whips and made them join the others in flight. Then, lifting the crest and helmet from his head, he was recognized by the Iberians, who rushed to attack him. Hamilcar's men and his sons thus gained a respite and escaped. He then turned to engage the Iberians, and, when they pressed him hard on all sides, he spurred his horse furiously and dashed into the waters of the Iber River and perished in the flood.

Upon Hamilcar's death, the Carthaginians invested his son-in-law, Hasdrubal, with the command, and Hasdrubal continued to subject the Iberian tribes to the domination of Carthage. Hasdrubal founded New Carthage, on the southern coast of Spain. After eight years, he was assassinated in his own house at night by a Celt in revenge for some private wrong, following which, Hannibal was invested with the command in Spain.

Hannibal had been sworn by his father, Hamilcar Barca, on their way to Spain, to forever have enmity toward Rome. Hamilcar Barca had taken Hannibal to the altar, and had him place his hand upon the sacrificial victim and swear an oath that he would never be a friend of Rome. Hannibal, therefore, inherited from his father a fierce, even bitter, hatred for Rome. Hannibal continued to bring the Iberian tribes into submission, and he laid siege to Saguntum, an old town with cyclopean walls, well defended. It was commanded by a pro-Roman faction, an anti-Carthaginian element. Rome, therefore, had, in effect, an enclave in Iberia. Saguntum, which held out bravely for eight months, finally fell, with the inevitable rapine and massacre that marked the end of long-disputed sieges in ancient times.

The Roman Senate then dispatched an envoy to Carthage to inquire as to whether Hannibal had acted on his own initiative or under the orders of Carthage. If Carthage disavowed the actions of Hannibal, then he would have to be surrendered to Roman authorities. But Carthage refused to surrender Hannibal, and the Carthaginian representatives then asked the Roman ambassador what his intentions were.

### "THE MOST MEMORABLE OF ALL WARS"

The Roman, who was named Marcus Fabius Buteo, placed his hand under his toga and said: "I hold in my hand both war and peace. Which will you choose?" The Carthaginians, after some consultation, returned and told the Roman that he himself should make the decision, whereupon Buteo, in

[61]

a very melodramatic gesture, withdrew his hand from his bosom and said, "I let fall war!" The Carthaginians responded, "We accept!" Thus, in this very casual manner there began, what Titus Livius, the Roman historian, referred to as "the most memorable of all wars," the Second Punic War.

There were three Barca brothers in Spain: Hannibal, Hasdrubal, and Mago. Mago was the youngest of the three brothers. Hasdrubal is not to be confused with the now-deceased son-in-law of Hamilcar Barca. These three brothers were known as "the Lion's Brood" throughout the army. They had prepared for the most audacious military move in history— an invasion of Italy by way of the forbidding, and hitherto untried, crossing over the Alps. No one had conceived that a whole army could be moved from the west, through the treacherous Alpine passes, and down into Italy. Such a course would be nothing less than sheer madness. But the intrepid Carthaginian, Hannibal—remember Napoleon had placed Hannibal higher than any other general in antiquity—this intrepid Carthaginian determined that where there was no way, he would make one. And he did.

In the spring of 218 B.C., with most of Iberia south of the Ebro River united behind him, Hannibal was ready for his departure. Hasdrubal was to remain in Spain to keep control over the Iberian tribes and to protect Carthaginian interests. Mago was to accompany Hannibal. In the early spring, Hannibal set out from Spain. He traversed the wild Pyrenees, the unknown land populated by barbarian savages in southern Gaul, and the fearsome Alps, and reached the plains of the Po River valley five months later. Polybius, the historian, says the actual passage over the Alps required fifteen days, and that Hannibal reached the valley of the Padus River with such of his army as had survived.

Hannibal had suffered great losses in men and horses and pack animals on the terrible journey over the Alps, during which he had been faced with storms, heavy snows, ice, traveling over treacherous precipices and through dangerous passes, confronted with heavy winds, rock slides, sub-zero temperatures, and miserable conditions of hunger. It had proved impossible to carry a full supply of food for so many thousands over such forbidding mountains. And much of what they did

[62]

bring was lost, together with the beasts of burden that carried it. Hannibal's men had quite abandoned all care for their health, and they suffered from the terrible neglect of proper attention to physical necessities. Whereas Hannibal had crossed the Rhone River with 46,000 men, he reached the valley of the Po with only 26,000. He had lost almost half of his army in the pass. Napoleon said of Hannibal, "He bought his battlefield at the price of half his army."

The survivors, through their terrible sufferings, had taken on the appearance of savages. Hannibal, therefore, spent his whole energies in restoring the spirits and the bodies of his men and their animals, among which were three dozen emaciated elephants. As soon as his men and their animals had sufficiently recuperated, Hannibal moved rapidly to attack the nearby towns, because now he was up against the tough, disciplined armies of Rome, and he felt it necessary to convince the Gauls of northern Italy that the Carthaginians were their deliverers against the Roman oppressor. He rapidly attacked the cities, put to the sword all who resisted him, and welcomed to his standard all who would join. These simple successes achieved their purpose, and thousands of Gauls in the surrounding area joined the ranks of Hannibal.

Two Roman consuls, in November 218 B.C., by the names of Publius Cornelius Scipio and Tiberius Sempronius Longus, advanced to grapple with Hannibal. Before their two armies could unite, Scipio bridged the Ticinus River, a tributary of the Po. He had gotten his troops across when Hannibal with his cavalry attacked and outflanked the Romans, who withdrew in confusion. But Hannibal followed hard upon their heels and captured six hundred of the Romans, whereupon two thousand Gauls revolted against their Roman masters and went over to Hannibal. Scipio had been severely wounded in the cavalry exchange, and this, together with the disturbing defection of two thousand Gauls, influenced his decision not to enter into a major battle with Hannibal until he had been joined with his fellow consul, Sempronius Longus.

Meanwhile, the nearby storage depot at Clastidium was betrayed into the hands of Hannibal by the commander of the town. Its granary served the Carthaginians well, as the cold winter of northern Italy set in.

[63]

Sempronius, then, in December 218 B.C., moved to join Scipio. Sempronius was an ambitious man. He was overly eager to give battle to Hannibal before his consular term expired. Hannibal, from the very beginning of the campaign, months and months prior thereto, had maintained an espionage system in Italy. And it was upon the suspected ambition of Sempronius Longus and his desire for a quick victory over Hannibal that Hannibal based his strategy. Hannibal knew how to make the terrain work for him and, knowing of Sempronius' desire for a quick victory, Hannibal set up an ambuscade and lured the whole Roman army across the Trebbia River and into the flat land where Hannibal's troops were drawn up for battle.

The trap was set. When the two armies came to hand-to-hand combat, Mago, the youngest of the three Barca brothers, emerged from a concealed area with one thousand horsemen and one thousand foot soldiers and fell upon the rear of the Roman armies. It was a set piece battle; a model of care and preparation; a triumph of strategy and tactical planning. The Romans were outgeneraled, and their army of forty thousand men was cut to pieces. Thousands of Romans and their allied forces were killed at the Trebbia River.

The cavalry encounter at the Ticinus River was but the first peremptory tap upon an ominous drum. But the rout and destruction of two Roman consular armies at the Trebbia River was no murmur of thunder in the distant hills. It was the deep rumble of an advancing avalanche that would shake Italy to its foundations.

Hannibal was wounded in the battle, but, despite his wound, he captured the large trading post of Victumulae, where he had been met with a hostile population of Gauls who opposed his attack upon the town. He routed the Gauls and completely exterminated them, because it was vital that the Gauls of northern Italy understand that fortune and freedom lay with joining the Carthaginian, and that he was even more merciless than the Romans if opposed.

Hannibal's relations with the Gauls were all-important for his success in the years ahead. He promised them, as he promised the men who had followed him from Spain, all of the lands they conquered, the booty of Italy, and the wealth of Rome. These were the men on whom he would have to depend

[64]

for the bulk of his army in the years to come, because he had no other manpower reserve. He was cut off from his base in Spain, and the Carthaginian government would never send him any supplies, never reinforce his army. These were the men, therefore, that he had to convince with his cunning, his intelligence, his skill, and his courage. At the same time, he had to seduce away from Rome her non-Roman Italian allies. If he could break up the confederation of Italian states, he would take away the manpower reserves upon which Rome had to depend, and he would isolate Rome.

In 217 B.C., two new consuls, Gaius Flaminius and Gnaeus Servilius Geminus were chosen. In view of the fact that both existing Roman consular armies had been destroyed at the battle of the Trebbia River, four new legions were levied.

I should state at this point that a Roman consular army consisted of two legions, each composed of from 4,200 to 6,000 men—if they were fully fleshed out—and 300 cavalry. A praetor had control over only one legion. Along with the legions, there was an equal number of Italian allies. Consequently, each Roman consul commanded two Roman legions, amounting to 10,000 to 12,000 men, together with an equal number of allied forces. Therefore, a consular army was made up of 20,000 to 25,000 men; two consular armies amounted to 40,000 to 50,000 men.

### Battle of Lake Trasimene

Flaminius was hostile toward the Roman Senate, and he also had quite a high opinion of his own military prowess because of a previous successful military campaign against the Gauls. Early in the spring of 217 B.C., Hannibal moved south into Etruria, but he chose a difficult route that the Romans would never have anticipated, crossing the marshes of the lower Arno River—marching three continuous days and nights through water. Only one of the thirty-seven elephants that had accompanied Hannibal across the Alps now survived, and Hannibal rode that elephant. It was here that Hannibal lost an eye. Juvenal, a Roman satirical poet, refers to Hannibal as the "one-eyed commander on his monstrous beast." Hannibal had stolen a brilliant tactical advantage over Flaminius and Geminus.

[65]

Far to the east, Geminus and his troops watched the roads and passes along the Adriatic. To the south, Flaminius waited at Arretium to bar the road to Rome. But Hannibal never intended to confront his enemies on a field not of his own choosing. He had bypassed Flaminius and moved toward Lake Trasimene, where his military genius quickly perceived that nature's terrain was ideal for a trap designed for slaughter.

On the border of Lake Trasimene, there was a narrow defile through which the road ran into a narrow valley. Hannibal arrived in advance of Flaminius and pitched his encampment on a hill at the far end of the valley. It was a steep hill and in full view of the entrance at the narrow defile. Hannibal stationed his Spanish and African infantry troops in front of the hill. And then, extending in order toward the entrance of the valley, he placed his Balearic slingers and his other light-arm troops under the cover of the hills. Farther along, and nearer the entrance, he stationed the Gauls and the cavalry.

Having made these elaborate preparations, Hannibal remained quiet and waited. The trap was set. Flaminius came along later in the day and saw Hannibal's camp on the hill at the other end of the valley. Inasmuch as darkness was coming on, Flaminius pitched his camp near the entrance to the valley. The next morning at daybreak, Flaminius moved his forces forward into the valley along the narrow defile and proceeded by the border of Lake Trasimene, with the idea in view that he would engage Hannibal at the far end of the valley. When the Roman troops were almost all within the valley, and the forward forces were almost upon Hannibal, he gave the signal to attack. When the trumpet sound reverberated through that valley, the trap was sprung. Hannibal's troops, who were lying in ambush behind the hills, delivered an assault upon the Roman columns, and the assault came everywhere at once—the front, the rear, and flank. Flaminius was taken by complete surprise. Hannibal's forces came down from the hills and attacked at all points simultaneously. The Romans were under the utmost distress and danger.

Polybius says in his history that fifteen thousand Romans died in the valley that day. The Romans who were caught in the narrow defile died in a most horrible manner. Pressed, as they were, into the lake by the Gauls and the Carthaginian cavalry, many of them, in their frantic terror, endeavored to swim with their armor on and were drowned. The greater number, however, waded into the lake as far as they could go and remained there with their heads above water. When the Carthaginian cavalry rode in after them, and they saw death staring them in the face, they held up their hands, offered to surrender, and begged for mercy. The Carthaginian cavalry dispatched them, except for those Romans who preferred to inflict the mortal blow on themselves. Flaminius, the consul, was killed. His body was never found. When the disastrous news reached Rome, the Romans were called to assemble. The praetor announced the gravity of the blow: "We have been beaten in a great battle."

Throughout the Punic wars, we shall see that it was the Roman Senate that led the Roman people through every trial to victory.

Mr. President, I yield the floor.

*Hannibal*

# CHAPTER 6

## Hannibal Devastates Italy, 218–203 B.C.

*June 15, 1993*

Mr. BYRD. Madam President, this is the sixth in my series of speeches on the history of the Roman people. Last week, we followed Hannibal on his terrible journey over the Alps and his invasion of Italy in 218 B.C., with a force of 26,000 men, having lost almost half of his army during the awful passage through the Alps. We then followed him to the battle at the Ticinus River in November of 218, where, in a battle with the Romans, he wounded the Roman consul Publius Cornelius Scipio. Then, we went with him to the battle at the Trebbia River in December of that year where he, through superior generalship, destroyed the consular armies of Scipio and Tiberius Sempronius Longus, in which battle the Romans lost 25,000 men killed and captured. He then went into the rich plain of Tuscany. At the battle of Lake Trasimene on June 22, 217 B.C., Hannibal created a trap in which fifteen thousand Romans were killed, including the consul Flaminius himself.

### FABIAN POLICY

Subsequent to the catastrophe at Lake Trasimene, the Roman Senate recognized the gravity of the situation and also recognized that it called for a drastic change. The Senate, therefore, arranged for the appointment of a dictator, whose term of office, as we have noted in an earlier speech, lasted only six months at the longest. The choice for dictator fell upon Quintus Fabius Maximus Verrucosus. He was a Roman of the old type, and he was the first to recognize that the religious ceremonies of the Roman people had been neglected. He, therefore, took steps to see that, in every respect, the divine element was not neglected, that the religious ceremonies would be kept, and that the rites and sacrifices would be observed. In this way, the morale of the people, to a great extent, was restored. Fabius also determined that there should be a new policy concerning Hannibal. It would later be called the "Fabian policy," a policy of harassment of Hannibal's army while avoiding an all-out battle.

Consequently, when Hannibal moved his army, Fabius followed along with his forces in the foothills of the Apennines, from whence he could send out raiding parties to harass Hannibal, but never engaging Hannibal in an all-out battle. This policy caused great consternation in Rome and in the Roman camp. In all previous campaigns, the Romans would seek out the enemy, march out and fight him, and, with the combination of their skill and discipline, bring him to his knees. We can, therefore, understand the resentment in Rome and in the Roman camp as they saw district after district in Italy go up in flames, while the Roman legions were compelled by the policy of Fabius to follow along slowly behind the Punic invader, never engaging him in battle.

Therefore, there was given to Fabius an agnomen—Cunctator, "the Delayer"—so that his name then was Quintus Fabius Maximus Verrucosus Cunctator, "the Delayer." Romans did not like this idea of not giving battle to the invader. But Fabius knew what he was doing, Hannibal knew what Fabius was doing, and Hannibal was concerned. Hannibal needed to fight great battles, and he needed to win spectacular victories in order to entice the allies away from Rome and to encourage them to join his own ranks. But the policy of Fabius would gradually wear Hannibal down. Hannibal knew this, because it would never fatally cost the Romans in manpower, while Hannibal's forces would, over time, dwindle away through attrition.

Then there came news that must have been encouraging to Hannibal, news that the Roman Senate did not intend to reappoint a dictator, and that Rome would revert to the consular system of having two consuls, each consul with an army made up of two legions, and each consul to exchange with the other consul on every other day the command of the army in the field. One of the Roman consuls that was chosen in 216 B.C. was Lucius Aemilius Paulus. He was a partisan of the aristocracy. He had been a consul before, and he had a good military record. The other consul, Gaius Terentius Varro, was a known demagog. He had managed to get into office by his defamatory attacks on Fabius, the dictator, and the Fabian policy of avoidance of battle with Hannibal.

Hannibal was compelled to capture Roman supply depots or live off the countryside in order to feed his army. Therefore, in the spring of 216 B.C., Hannibal and his army began to move. He moved southward, and crossing the Aufidus River, descended upon the town of Cannae. Cannae was one of the original Roman grain depots, and one from which the Romans had been supplying their armies. By seizing Cannae, Hannibal, therefore, deprived the Romans of a main source of supply, while at the same time, providing a more than adequate supply of food for his own army.

BATTLE OF CANNAE

The Roman Senate then ordered Paulus and Varro, together with the proconsuls, and the consuls of the previous year, Atilius and Servilius Geminus, to engage the Punic invader in battle and to retake the town of Cannae. Toward the end of July of that year, 216 B.C., therefore, these several Roman armies converged on the town of Cannae.

Hannibal, having been the first to arrive, had had an opportunity to carefully examine the area all around Cannae and the Aufidus River, and had selected a level plain on which to do battle, as this would give his cavalry, his Numidian horsemen, an opportunity to demonstrate their superiority over the Roman allied cavalry.

Paulus and Varro and Servilius and Atilius were late in arriving; they were unfamiliar with the grounds, and they arrived after a long march. But Paulus, being in command that day, and having had considerable experience in military matters, saw clearly that the level plain was advantageous to a cavalry action. He, therefore, cautioned Varro that it would be more advantageous to the Roman legions and their allies to move to hillier ground. This was the first day in which the opposing armies had had an opportunity to view one another from a distance.

On the next day, the second day after the armies had come within sight of one another, Varro was in command. He did not agree with Paulus that the armies should be moved to higher and more hilly ground. He would have nothing to do with anything that savored of Fabius, the Delayer. Any talk of hillier ground made him all the more determined to move down on the plain. Therefore, he decided to move the armies down on the plain behind the hill of Cannae.

On the third day, Paulus was again in command. The two camps, which had been set up opposing one another, about two miles apart, being on the east side of the river, Hannibal moved over on the west side and so did Paulus. But Paulus did not accept the opportunity to do battle with Hannibal.

On the fourth day, it was Varro's turn again to take the command. Shortly after sunrise, on August 2, 216 B.C., he began to move his forces out of camp and onto the field. As the Romans were drawing up their battle formation, Hannibal placed his forces into the pattern that he had designed for them. The Numidian cavalry was stationed on the far right of the Carthaginian center. The heavy cavalry, consisting of Carthaginians, was stationed on the far left, near the Aufidus River. It was noticeable that the Carthaginian center was drawn forward in a curious crescent-shaped formation, with the "cusp" or convex of the crescent projecting toward the enemy. Varro, in drawing up his forces, placed his allied cavalry on the Roman left and the Roman cavalry on the Roman right. Varro did not establish any wings on this occasion. He packed all of the Roman legions and the allied infantry into one dense formation, expecting that the weight of the armored legions would punch a hole a thousand yards wide right through Hannibal's center.

Hannibal stationed his Carthaginian and Libyan heavy infantry as wings to the left and to the right of the center. These Carthaginians and Libyans were his more experienced veterans, and they were equipped with swords and shields that had been taken from the Romans at Lake Trasimene.

[72]

Hannibal opened the battle proper with his Gauls and Spaniards in the crescent center—they were his swordsmen—leaving the Carthaginian and Libyan heavy infantry as reserves on both wings where they formed rectangles, flanking the projecting crescent. Livius says that both armies pushed straight ahead. The Roman cavalry on the flank beside the river was promptly overwhelmed and defeated and it turned and fled. Hannibal's Numidian cavalry promptly engaged the allied cavalry on the opposite wing. Slowly but surely, the cusp of the crescent-shaped center yielded and fell back, a little more, and then a little more, until it became a straightened line, and then an indentation, and then a concave crescent. All the while, the densely packed legions and their allies, having been deprived of the mobility which the open formation normally gave them, began to pour in, one behind another, like a stream of armor bursting through a collapsing dike. And yet, on either side of the yielding center, the Carthaginian heavy infantry stood firm. So far, the Carthaginian heavy infantry on both sides of the center had taken no part in the battle.

The Numidian cavalry had triumphed over the allied cavalry and was pursuing the enemy wherever it scattered. All the while, the Roman and allied legions were continuing to drive deeper into Hannibal's center. Then a trumpet sounded, and the moment had arrived. Hannibal's tactic of double envelopment of the Roman legions was complete! The two Carthaginian sides moved in. The convex center had now become a U-shaped crescent. The rectangles of heavy infantry projected beyond the U-shaped center like banks enclosing a river of moving armor. The Carthaginian heavy cavalry, which had by now completely routed the Roman cavalry and was returning, moved to the center and attacked the Roman legions from the rear. The Numidian cavalry did the same. To complete the terrible trap, the Roman legions—this great mass of men closely packed, so close they could no longer use their weapons—found that their rear lines were being assailed. Completely encircled now, since the Gauls and the Spaniards in the collapsing crescent continued to fight on, ferociously contesting every foot of ground, the Romans and their allies were totally stricken, as the two Carthaginian sides moved in like the two sides of an enfolding vise.

[73]

On that hot August afternoon, the plain of Cannae became a slaughter field. It was the greatest defeat ever inflicted on the Romans. Plutarch and Appian tell us that fifty thousand Romans were killed. Quintilian says sixty thousand. Polybius says seventy thousand. The consul Lucius Aemilius Paulus was killed. Varro, the man who was responsible for the disaster, had fled. In addition to Paulus, the two proconsuls, Servilius and Atilius, died; eighty senators, two quaestors—state treasurers—twenty-nine military tribunes, over half the total of those scions of noble Roman blood died in the battle of Cannae that afternoon.

The volume of loot that the Carthaginians gathered at the Roman camp and on the field of battle was colossal—arms, armor, silver and gold, horse trappings, horses and baggage. Paulus Orosius, a historian of the late fourth and early fifth centuries A.D., who was highly regarded by St. Augustine, tells us that "in no other battle of the Punic War were the Romans so close to annihilation," and that Hannibal "sent to Carthage, as proof of his victory, three pecks of gold rings that he had pulled from the hands of the slain Roman knights and senators."

ROME'S IRON DETERMINATION

Hannibal sent ten of the Roman captives who had been taken prisoner, together with a Carthaginian noble, Carthalo, to Rome. Carthalo was to offer to ransom the prisoners taken at the battle of Cannae. If Hannibal had any high expectations, he was bound to be disappointed. Carthalo was not allowed to enter Rome and was told to be clear of the city's territory before nightfall. If Hannibal had hoped by his magnanimity to determine the state of Roman morale, the Roman Senate was equally determined that Hannibal should learn that there had been no weakening of morale.

Rome then showed its iron mood. The Roman Senate doubled the war tax and provided that slaves should be bought from their owners on condition of their enlistment into the Roman legions. Prisoners were to be removed from the jails on condition that they join the legions. The Senate provided that all artisans and craftsmen be conscripted into the manufacture of armaments. The Roman Senate showed its teeth.

[74]

Fabius was reinstituted as dictator, and once more he inaugurated the old Roman code. He became, again, the rock upon which Roman morale was strengthened, and was placed in charge, again, of the defense of the country. Through his policy, the Fabian policy, Hannibal would never again be given the opportunity to deal a catastrophic blow to the Roman armies such as they suffered on the field of Cannae that afternoon in August 216 B.C.

If, thereafter, the Romans were rash enough to engage Hannibal in battle or to accept an engagement in battle through a challenge by Hannibal, they would learn the usual bloody lesson. Such a lesson was taught in the year 209 B.C., at Herdonia, where Fulvius Centumalus, a proconsul, was encamped against the town of Herdonia, which was controlled by pro-Carthaginian Italians. Hannibal heard of this threat and, by forced marches, came up out of Bruttium and engaged the Roman legions that were besieging the town. While his cavalry attacked the legions from the rear, Hannibal's infantry struck from the front and the flanks. The outcome was another one of those mortifying defeats which, until the end of the war, made every Roman general tremble.

Meanwhile, in 207 B.C., Hannibal's brother, Hasdrubal, was victorious over two Roman consular armies in Spain. Both armies were destroyed. The two consuls were killed, and they were both Scipios.

Hasdrubal, therefore, prepared to depart from Spain and join Hannibal in Italy, because only by a junction of the two armies and a complete defeat of the Romans could the goal of the long war be achieved. Hasdrubal crossed the Alps with his army, as had Hannibal eleven years earlier. But Hasdrubal did not encounter the same difficulties that plagued Hannibal. Hasdrubal started his journey at a different time, after the snows had melted, and he, apparently, took a pass that was distinct from the one that Hannibal had chosen, and to the north of it.

Hasdrubal descended into Italy and moved south like an ominous cloud over the land of Italy. Communications, of course, in that ancient time were so poor that Hannibal in the south, in Apulia, only had an idea that Hasdrubal should by this time be across the Alps. Hasdrubal, already in Italy, knew only that Hannibal was somewhere in the south of Italy, but he did not know exactly where. It was important, therefore, that Hasdrubal get information to Hannibal quickly as to Hasdrubal's location and a suggested rendezvous.

Hasdrubal by this time had reached Ariminum, shown as Rimini on the map, a seaport on the Adriatic coast of Italy, it being his intention to go from there to Narnia in Umbria. He prepared a letter for delivery to Hannibal somewhere in south Italy. Hasdrubal chose six horsemen—two Numidians and four Gauls—to carry the message through the land of Italy, which was teeming with Roman and allied troops. In this letter, Hasdrubal apparently not only indicated to Hannibal the location of the rendezvous, where the two armies were to join and fight the critical battle of Italy, but also included the information concerning his current location and the composition of his entire army.

Disaster befell the messengers. They were intercepted, and fortune took a hand. The letter was immediately transmitted to the Roman consul in the south, Claudius Nero, and he acted with masterly speed and decisiveness. Setting out from Apulia, where his army faced off Hannibal, and leaving thirty thousand Roman and allied troops under the command of Catius, a legate, Nero started under cover of night on a forced march north to join the other consul and his army. Nero knew two things. Nero knew the location of Hasdrubal's army, and the location of the rendezvous at which Hasdrubal had proposed to meet his brother Hannibal and fuse their two armies. Nero also knew that Hannibal did not know the location of Hasdrubal or the location of the proposed rendezvous. Nero made a forced march of seven days and arrived in the camp of his fellow consul, Marcus Livius Salinator, under cover of darkness.

Hasdrubal was unaware of the presence of two consuls until he went out with a small escort in front of the Roman lines and noticed strange horses, lean horses, more horses than before. He then sent out a small party to scour the area and to listen whether there were two bugle calls or one. It was reported back to Hasdrubal that there were, in fact, three bugle calls. Hasdrubal then knew that his worst fears were true. There were two consuls and their armies, and the third bugle

[76]

call meant that a Roman praetor, Porcius Licinus, was also present with an army. Apprehensive, therefore, Hasdrubal gave orders to his troops to pack their baggage in silence, stoke the fires, and leave camp at night.

In the confusion and the disorder, unfortunately, Hasdrubal's guides were not watched carefully and they slipped away. Hasdrubal ordered his men to follow the River Metaurus, but, without the guides, Hasdrubal and his army wandered blindly along the twists and turns and wasted a day in an effort to find a ford where he could cross the river. This gave the enemy the opportunity to overtake him.

There was a fierce battle, and both sides lost heavily. Hasdrubal's elephants caused great disorder among the Romans and forced their columns to retreat. But as the battle grew more fierce and the violence more great and the clamor louder, the elephants became disoriented and raged from one side to the other, like a ship without rudders in a storm. When they began to charge their own lines, as though they had forgotten to whom they belonged, their drivers had to kill them.

Time after time, Hasdrubal displayed great courage and encouraged his men to rally. Again and again, he led them into danger by his own personal example. More than once, he turned his soldiers in flight and restored the battle which had been abandoned. Finally, when it was no longer doubtful as to which side would be the victor, Hasdrubal spurred his horse into the Roman lines and died, fighting in a manner worthy of his illustrious father, Hamilcar Barca, and his inimitable brother, Hannibal.

Nero, the next night, began the journey back to Apulia, and arrived at the Roman camp in southern Italy after six days, making the return trip faster than when he had gone north.

Meanwhile, Hannibal had been unaware of the absence of Nero for two weeks, together with the six thousand legionnaires and one thousand cavalrymen that had been taken by Nero north when he joined Livius. Hannibal was also unaware of the disaster that had befallen his brother until Roman cavalrymen spurred their horses up to the Carthaginian sentries at night, and tossed a dark object into their midst. When it was

[77]

brought to Hannibal in his tent, he took one look and said, "I see there the fate of Carthage." It was the head of his dead brother, Hasdrubal.

Hannibal then decamped and took his remaining forces into Bruttium, the toe of Italy, the wild and mountainous area from which he had drawn most of his recruits in recent years, and where he was in possession of two small seaports, the seaport of Locri and the seaport of Croton.

Following the battle of the Metaurus, which was one of the decisive battles of the world, Hannibal's last chance and last hope of ever conquering Rome were gone. Yet, from that year of 207 B.C., to the year 203 B.C., Hannibal remained in Italy unconquered.

Meanwhile, the main theater of war had shifted to Spain where Publius Cornelius Scipio—son of the Scipio who had been wounded at the Ticinus River in 218 B.C.—who, incidentally, would become the conqueror of Hannibal at Zama in the year 202 B.C., and be given the surname or agnomen, "Africanus," was winning victories. He was, through his victories in Spain over Hannibal's brother Mago, wresting control of Spain out of the hands of the Carthaginians.

The years, meanwhile, had taken their toll on Hannibal's army. No longer did he have the brilliant officers and experienced warriors and superb Numidian cavalrymen who had followed him in the early battles and who had adorned his magnificent exploits in the earlier years. His army now was virtually a different army and, in any other hands, it would not have posed a threat to Rome. But it was the dreaded name of Hannibal that continued to tie down so many thousands of Romans.

Scipio, in the year 204 B.C., moved with his legions from Spain to North Africa where he attacked Carthage, and in 203 B.C., Hannibal was recalled from Italy to Carthage to do battle with Scipio.

Polybius informs us that Hannibal, upon being recalled, was bitter. "So now they are recalling me," he said of his government, which "for years" had refused him "money and reinforcements." He embarked from the little seaport of Croton. Leaving Italy, he looked back upon that land in which he had fought so many bloody battles and in which he had remained unconquered for sixteen turbulent years, and as it faded forever in the distance behind him, he knew in his heart that the cause for which he had suffered so long, was lost.

The historian states that no native ever left his own native land with greater chagrin and disappointment and regret than did Hannibal in leaving the enemy country of Italy in 203 B.C.

The battle of Zama was fought in the year 202 B.C. Scipio defeated Hannibal. Hannibal's defeat can mainly be ascribed to his lack of cavalry. He had eighty elephants which became unmanageable, but inasmuch as he had little cavalry, he had to use the elephants. Polybius tells us that Hannibal did everything that a good and experienced general was supposed to do, and that the excellence of his troop dispositions could not have been surpassed.

Terms were entered into between Scipio and Hannibal, and Hannibal recommended to the Carthaginian government that the government agree to the terms. A treaty was signed in the year 201 B.C.

Cornelius Nepos, a first-century B.C. Roman historian, in writing of the final years of Hannibal's life, states that Hannibal had exiled himself in the dominions of King Prusias of Bithynia, when the Romans accidentally heard of his whereabouts. The conscript fathers, who thought that they would never be free from plots as long as Hannibal was alive, sent ambassadors to Bithynia, to request the king not to keep their bitterest enemy with him, but to deliver him up to them. Prusias did not dare to refuse; he made some opposition, however, to one point, begging them not to require of him what was contrary to the rights of hospitality, saying that they themselves might make Hannibal prisoner, if they would, as they could easily find out the place where he was. Hannibal, indeed, confined himself to one place, living in a fortress which had been given him by the king. When the Roman ambassadors found and surrounded his house with a number of men, a slave, looking out at a gate, told Hannibal that several armed men were to be seen, contrary to what was usual. Hannibal commanded him to go around to all the gates of the castle, and bring him word immediately whether it was beset in the same way on all sides. The slave having soon reported that it was and informed him that all the passages were secured, he felt certain that it was no accidental occurrence, but that his person was menaced, and that his life was no longer to be preserved. That he might not part with his life, however, at the pleasure of another, Hannibal took poison, which he had been accustomed always to carry with him in a secret compartment of a finger ring. Lucius Quintius Flaminius, a Roman consul, entered the building only to find that the great Carthaginian, who had so often foiled and eluded the Roman legions in life, had escaped them again—this time in death.

Regardless of the great achievements of this master strategist and technician on the battlefield, Hannibal was never able to break the strength of the Roman Senate. If it had been any nation other than Rome, his victories would have brought that nation to its knees. Livy, the Roman historian, said, "No other nation could have suffered such a tremendous disaster and not been destroyed." In one afternoon at Cannae, there were more Romans killed than there were soldiers lost by the United States in the entire eight years of the Vietnam war.

It was the Roman Senate that demonstrated the superb quality of stability and led the Romans and their allies to ultimate victory. The Hannibalic war had cost Rome terribly in treasury and in men. The intrepid Carthaginian had roamed the land of Italy, burning the towns and cities, ravishing and plundering the countryside, devastating the Roman legions, exacting an awful price from Rome in treasure and in blood. Through it all, it was the Roman Senate that led the people to final victory.

Senators, as I come to the conclusion of my remarks, I call attention to the fact that today is the 778th anniversary of the Magna Carta. That charter was signed by King John in the year 1215 on June 15 in the meadow of Runnymede beside the Thames River. This is significant because it was at Runnymede that the governed demanded that the king of England recognize certain rights of the governed. The barons, of course, were interested in protecting their own rights, but, in doing so, they also protected the rights of free men. They demanded of the sovereign—the executive—that he recognize his own limitations and that he also recognize their rights. The barons broke the tyranny of royal absolutism. The charter, in its sixty-three provisions, provided for a committee of nobles who would call the king to account if he failed to live up to the charter. That was the foundation, the bedrock of American constitutional representative democracy. The Magna Carta came into its full flowering in 1689 when William and Mary became the two joint sovereigns in England.

The Roman Senate had the same opportunity as did the English barons to exact from the sovereign (the executive) an assurance of the rights and liberties of the people. For several hundred years, during the early and middle republic, the Roman Senate was supreme. But it lost its nerve and voluntarily ceded away its powers. It chose, in time, to yield its authority to military dictators and, later, to the emperors. The Senate then began to recede and decline, and the executive became all powerful.

The speeches I have been making concern, in the final analysis, the unwisdom of a line-item veto. With these two histories as background—the history of the rise and fall of the Roman republic, and the history of Magna Carta and the long struggle by English parliaments against tyrannical monarchs—I see many senators contemplating following the example of the Roman Senate, which surrendered its powers to an all-powerful executive, and, in doing so, became subordinate to the executive.

We should, instead, follow the example of the barons at Runnymede and maintain control of the purse, thus protecting the liberties and rights of the people and retaining limitations, as our English forebears did, upon the executive. But instead of following that principle, I am afraid we may be contemplating, with the line-item veto, the example of the Roman Senate: losing our nerve and shifting the power of the people, through their elected representatives, to an all-powerful executive. If we do that, then we, the senators and representatives of today, will be held accountable by our children and our children's children, just as history must hold the Roman Senate largely accountable, in the final analysis, for the decline and fall of the Roman republic.

I yield the floor.

*Destruction of Carthage*

# CHAPTER 7

# Rome Triumphant, 202–133 B.C.

*June 22, 1993*

Mr. BYRD. Mr. President, this is the seventh in my series of speeches on the so-called line-item veto.

Last week, we followed Hannibal, the Carthaginian general, to the battle of Cannae, which occurred on August 2, 216 B.C. We also followed Hannibal to the battle of Zama in North Africa, in 202 B.C.

### ONE OF THE GREATEST BATTLES OF ANTIQUITY

At the battle of Cannae, Hannibal inflicted the greatest defeat ever suffered by the Romans and their allies. Broadly speaking, Rome's allies were of two classes: one, the Latin allies; and, two, the Federated Italian States, which were spread throughout the Italian peninsula. The allies did not serve within the Roman legions; they formed separate detachments of cavalry and foot soldiers to serve under the control of the Roman consuls or other Roman officers commanding the legions. The allies constituted scores of communities, both tribal and city, each of which had its own special treaty with Rome. The allied communities raised their own detachments of soldiers and horsemen, and equipped their own armies, but they received their subsistence from Rome and shared equally with the Romans in the distribution of spoils from the wars.

The battle of Cannae was one of the greatest battles of antiquity, and it was the bloodiest of all Roman defeats. At Cannae, the consummate military genius of Hannibal was displayed, and his masterly tactics on that occasion have found admirers among the great commanders in all of the subsequent ages. He was able to win a victory there over vastly superior numbers

[ 83 ]

by forcing the Roman army to "jam" itself. He forced it to crowd itself densely into a struggling, helpless mass—a mass which was shut in on all sides, a mass upon which every blow told, a mass which could give but few blows in return.

In one afternoon, the Romans and their allies lost more men on the slaughter field at Cannae than the United States lost during the entire eight years of the war in Vietnam. A terrible sinking feeling of utter despair descended like a cloud upon Roman citizens when they heard the awful news of the carnage and destruction dealt by this latest blow at the hands of Hannibal. Eighty senators were killed, along with the consul Paulus, the proconsuls Atilius and Servilius, two quaestors, a former master of the horse, and twenty-nine military tribunes. Yet, the reaction of the Roman Senate was to display its iron mood. The stamina of the Romans and the resiliency of the Roman political system were such that they were able to endure thirteen additional years of devastation and ruin dealt by Hannibal before he left Italy in 203 B.C. to be defeated at the battle of Zama in 202 B.C. by the Roman consul Publius Cornelius Scipio, surnamed Africanus.

The Second Punic War had ended, and, yet, there was hardly a mother within the walls of Rome who had not suffered the loss of a brother, a son, a father, or a husband. A heavy tribute had been levied upon the manpower of Rome, and the wastage of blood in the struggle was best seen in the reduced numbers of men available for military service in the legions. The federated allies had undoubtedly suffered losses just as great. The greatest allied losses fell upon southern Italy, where, year after year, the fields were laid waste and villages devastated by the opposing armies until the rural population had almost disappeared, the land had become a virtual wilderness, and many towns had fallen into decay. It was a struggle that called forth a recrudescence of the old Roman virtues of courage, self sacrifice, patriotism, and religious devotion.

We saw last week that the Roman dictator, Fabius Maximus, was chosen in 217 B.C., following the disastrous defeat of Flaminius at Lake Trasimene on June 22 of that same year. We saw Fabius take steps to renew the religious ceremonies and to assure that the divine element would not be neglected. By so doing, Maximus restored the morale of the Roman people.

[84]

We also witnessed the rugged patriotism of the Roman Senate when it refused the offer of Hannibal to ransom Roman soldiers taken prisoner at Cannae.

## THE ROMAN SENATE'S ZENITH

The Roman Senate had reached its zenith. It had emerged from the Second Punic War more powerful than ever. And even though the will of the people was theoretically sovereign after the passage of the Hortensian law in 287 B.C., from that time to the tribunate of Tiberius Sempronius Gracchus in 133 B.C., the Senate exercised a practically unchallenged control over the Roman state. The Senate was able to guide or to nullify the actions of the Roman magistrates, the tribunate, and the assemblies. It assigned to the consuls their spheres of duty. It allotted to the other magistrates their commands. And all contracts that were let by the censors were only valid if they were approved by the Roman Senate. The Senate continued to exercise its absolute control over all expenditures from the public treasury, and, through its influence over the magistrates and the tribunes, the Senate was able to control the legislative and the elective functions of the comitia.

The treaty that ended the Second Punic War had imposed upon Carthage the restriction that she could not make war anywhere without the consent of Rome. This had the effect of making Carthage a client of Rome. At the same time, Masinissa, a strong Numidian ruler, was installed as a loyal Roman client on the western and southern boundaries of Carthage. The Romans continued, perhaps exaggeratedly, to fear and suspect their former enemy, and they were, therefore, prepared to seize upon any pretext that would serve as an excuse for the destruction of Carthage. The opportunity came through the machinations of Masinissa. The Numidian chieftain, knowing the restrictions imposed upon Carthage by her treaty with Rome, and understanding the attitude of Rome toward Carthage, attacked Punic territory frequently.

Under the treaty, the Carthaginians, of course, could do nothing but appeal to Rome, but the numerous commissions that were sent out by the Roman Senate to investigate the complaints of frontier violations invariably decided in favor of Masinissa. One member of a commission sent out to resolve such a border

[85]

dispute in 157 B.C. was Marcus Porcius Cato the Elder. Cato was still obsessed with the fear that the invasion of Hannibal had inspired in his early life, and Cato returned from his mission to Carthage filled with alarm at the wealth and the growing prosperity and strength of Carthage, which he considered to be a deadly rival of Rome. He, therefore, bent all of his energies toward accomplishing the downfall of Carthage, and, in all of his succeeding years, he concluded all of his speeches in the Roman Senate with the words, "Carthage must be destroyed."

Friction with Masinissa resulted in a chain of events that led ultimately to the delivery of an ultimatum by Rome to the Carthaginians to abandon their city and to resettle at least ten miles from the seacoast. This was practically a death sentence to the ancient mercantile city. The Carthaginians decided upon a last-ditch defense of Punic interests. Their weapons had been taken from them by the Romans earlier. They, therefore, improvised weapons, manned the city's walls, and defied the Romans. Thus, the Third Punic War began in 149 B.C.

THIRD PUNIC WAR

For two years, the Romans, because of the incompetency of their commanders, and also because of the heroic and spirited defense of the city, accomplished little. In 147 B.C., Publius Cornelius Scipio Aemilianus, the adopted grandson of Scipio Africanus the Elder, was chosen consul. He immediately went about defeating the Carthaginians in the field, and energetically besieged the city. In the spring of 146 B.C., Scipio Aemilianus captured Carthage after a terrible struggle in the streets and in house-to-house fighting throughout the city.

The Carthaginian survivors, numbering about fifty thousand, were sold into slavery, and their city was leveled to the ground. The site upon which the city had stood was declared accursed. Carthage was no more. The conquered territory was formed into a Roman province called Africa.

In the same year of 146 B.C., which witnessed the destruction of Carthage, the Greek city of Corinth was sacked and burned by the Roman consul, Lucius Mummius, surnamed Achaicus. The art treasures of the city were carried off to Rome, and the inhabitants, like the inhabitants of Carthage, were sold into slavery. The other Greek cities entered into individual relations with Rome; some, like Sparta and Athens, as Roman allies; others were made subject and tributary.

Mr. President, time precludes me from making more than a passing reference to the Macedonian and Syrian wars and other wars from which Rome emerged victorious. In 168 B.C., the Roman consul, Lucius Aemilius Paulus, surnamed Macedonicus, won a complete victory over King Perseus of Macedonia at the battle of Pydna. Perseus was taken to Rome, where he was treated with scorn and ignominy, and he died there in captivity. The Macedonian kingdom, therefore, was brought to an end in 168 B.C.

During the Third Macedonian War, the Syrian king, Antiochus IV, Epiphanes, invaded Egypt. The Roman Senate, following the battle of Pydna, dispatched an ambassador, Gaius Popillius Laenas, to call upon Antiochus and to urge him to withdraw from Egypt. Popillius met with Antiochus at Alexandria, and Popillius delivered to Antiochus the message from the Roman Senate urging him to withdraw from Egypt. The Syrian king asked for time to consider. The Roman drew a circle around the Syrian king and bade him to answer before he left the spot. Antiochus yielded and pulled his troops out of Egypt.

Cisalpine Gaul, that area of north Italy on the southern side of the Alps bordering the Po River, had been largely lost to Rome during the Hannibalic invasion, but it was recovered by wars.

In Spain, Scipio Aemilianus, the destroyer of Carthage, destroyed Numantia in 133 B.C., and the Carthaginian territory in Spain was organized by Rome into two provinces, Hither Spain and Farther Spain.

In that same year of 133 B.C., the king of Pergamum, Attalus III, surnamed Philometor, died, the last of his line. In his will, he made Rome the heir to his kingdom. The kingdom of Pergamum was formed into a new province, the province of Asia. The occupation of this kingdom made Rome the mistress of both shores of the Aegean Sea and provided a convenient bridgehead for Rome for further advances eastward.

Mr. President, when Rome embarked on the First Punic War in 264 B.C., no Roman soldier had ever set foot out of Italy.

But between 264 B.C. and 133 B.C., as we have seen, Rome became supreme throughout the Mediterranean world.

A SENSE OF DESTINY

From the earliest times, the Romans had believed that Rome had a providential destiny, smiled upon by the gods. The individual Roman believed in that sense of purpose for his country, and he also believed that it was his personal duty and mission to give his life, if necessary, toward the fulfillment of that providential destiny for his country.

I also mentioned in one of my earlier speeches that there were many parallels between the history of the Romans and the history of America. And, as we have witnessed this territorial expansion by Rome between the years 264 B.C. and 133 B.C., it is evident that one of these parallels was that strong sense of national destiny.

From the very beginning of our own history, the uniqueness of the American national mission has received religious and secular explanations. As senators will recall from our study of American history, John Winthrop, in a sermon in 1630, exhorted his fellow travelers to New England: "Men shall say of succeeding plantations, the Lord make it like that of New England. . . . For we must consider that we shall be as a city upon a hill, the eyes of all people upon us."

We will also remember that, after 200 years of westward expansion, which brought them to Missouri and Iowa, Americans perceived their destined goal. The whole breadth of the continent was to be theirs! It was for a man by the name of John L. O'Sullivan, a New York journalist, to capture this mood in one sentence. He wrote in 1845—"Nothing must interfere with the fulfillment of our manifest destiny to overspread the continent allotted by Providence for the free development of our yearly multiplying millions."

Mr. President, for all of its existence, the United States Senate has been the principal national forum for applying this powerful sense of destiny to the fundamental issues that have faced generations of Americans. And it is not too far from reality to understand what the historians have meant, when they have identified the Senate's "Golden Age"—that period beginning in the second quarter of the nineteenth century—with the start

[ 88 ]

of fierce debates over the concept of our nation's structure and destiny. But whether the national destiny is to be defined as "territorial expansion," in the nineteenth-century sense, or as the advancement of science and commerce, individual liberty, human rights, economic opportunity, or space exploration and travel, the United States Senate has played an indispensable role, as did the Roman Senate two thousand years ago.

Mr. President, the century that began with the year 133 B.C. has often been referred to as the period of the Roman Revolution. It was an era of increasingly bitter strife that erupted into bloody civil wars, which ultimately destroyed government by oligarchy, brought about the end of the Roman republic, and replaced it with a disguised form of monarchy. At this point, I again refer to the Magna Carta, which was signed on June 15, 1215.

At Runnymede, for the first time in recorded history, representatives of the governed—in this case, the English barons— called upon the royal executive, King John of England, to account for his imperious behavior, and they coerced him into signing the agreement which ever after required him to recognize limitations upon his royal power. Out of that deed was born, over a period of long and bloody centuries, the idea and the reality of representative government, government in which there were limitations on the powers of those who governed.

The Magna Carta is viewed as the basic keystone document in the Anglo-Saxon heritage of constitutional and limited government. It is also viewed as the underlying foundation of our American heritage, of the right of the governed to place limitations on the powers of government officials, especially the chief executive.

Conversely, as the Roman Senate slowly but surely lost its will to shoulder its responsibility to act as a check upon the executive, more and more, the Roman Senate ceded power into the hands of those executives, or imperators—emperors, as they were later called—who finally, in fact, took power into their own hands.

This ceding, or transfer, of power into the hands of dictators and emperors resulted from a loss of will and courage by the Roman Senate, and it reflected the slow decadence and the agonizingly prolonged decline that Rome experienced as the republic collapsed and the empire emerged.

What has all of this to do with the line-item veto? What does Roman history have to do with the line-item veto? Where is the relevancy? Well, Robert C. Byrd is not the only individual who has detected a relevancy between the line-item veto and Roman history. The great Montesquieu—author and philosopher—wrote, as we very well know, *The Persian Letters* and *The Spirit of the Laws*.

But perhaps not many people know that Montesquieu also wrote a history of the Roman people—of their greatness and their decline. He was intrigued by the Romans and their history. He also visited the various political divisions in Europe and sojourned for a time in England.

It was the history of the contemporary institutions of England, together with Roman history, that most influenced Montesquieu in his political philosophy concerning the separation of powers and checks and balances. Montesquieu's philosophy had a great impact upon the framers of the United States Constitution. Those men who met in Philadelphia in the summer of 1787 well knew about Montesquieu and his philosophy of divided powers and checks and balances, and they drove that linchpin right into the center of the Constitution. The power of the purse, of course, is the mainspring in that constitutional system of checks and balances.

What is the relevancy of Roman history? To put it simply and elementally, by delivering the line-item veto into the hands of a president—any president, Republican or Democrat or Independent—the United States Senate will have set its foot on the same road to decline, subservience, impotence, and feebleness that the Roman Senate followed in its own descent into ignominy, cowardice, and oblivion.

Mr. President, will we stay with the spirit of Runnymede? Or will we go the way of Imperial Rome?

Mr. President, I yield the floor.

*History is the witness that testifies to the passing of time; it illuminates reality, vitalizes memory, provides guidance in daily life, and brings us the tidings of antiquity.*

Marcus Tullius Cicero

ᏬᎧᏔᎧ

*There is the moral of all human tales;*
*'Tis but the same rehearsal of the past,*
*First freedom, and then Glory—when that fails,*
*Wealth, vice, corruption,—barbarism at last.*
*And History, with all her volumes vast,*
*Hath but one page,—*

Lord Byron, *Childe Harold's Pilgrimage*

ᏬᎧᏔᎧ

*[I]f one is to gain wisdom by virtue of his long years of life, how much more will he gain in wisdom if he studies the lives of great men? If he studies history as it bridges the centuries of time, he then becomes the recipient, the beneficiary of the wisdom of hundreds of lifetimes stretching back into the dim mists of antiquity. That is why we are told to study history. [page 6]*

*Tiberius Gracchus Closes the Temple of Saturn*

*Gaius Gracchus, Tribune of the People*

# CHAPTER 8

## Erosion of Senate Authority

*June 29, 1993*

Mr. BYRD. Madam President, this is the eighth in my series of speeches on the Roman Senate and the Roman constitutional system. Last week, I spoke of the devastation wreaked by Hannibal's army upon Italy during the Second Punic War. For sixteen years, Hannibal maintained the war in Italy without once releasing his army from service in the field. He kept control of the thousands of men without any sign of disaffection toward himself or toward each other, even though he had troops in his army of many nationalities. He had Libyans, Iberians, Gauls, Carthaginians, Ligurians, Bruttians, Greeks, and Numidians, who had nothing in common with each other, neither laws nor customs nor language. Yet, the skill of this commander was such that in spite of these differences, so manifold and so wide, there was never one word of disobedience to his command or to his single iron will.

Unlike Caesar, Alexander, and Pyrrhus, Hannibal was never the subject of an assassination plot or even a hint of conspiracy on the part of his troops. Also unlike Alexander, Hannibal was virtually forsaken by his native country of Carthage, receiving no reinforcements, or very few at best, and no money from his homeland. Yet, Hannibal's polyglot army had to be paid, and so he plundered the countryside and the ancient shrines, where offerings of gold and silver dating from immemorial times were used to pay his mercenaries.

### ROMAN VENGEANCE

The losses of the Romans, as we have witnessed, had been frightful. Many of Rome's elite had been wiped out, and much

[93]

of the wealth of Italy—its livestock, its crops, its cultivated land, its houses and equipment—was destroyed over vast areas, especially in southern Italy. Yet, the unyielding determination of the Senate and the iron discipline of the Roman people persevered.

Any city that cooperated with Hannibal could expect no mercy but only the most severe punishment for its infidelity to Rome. I will cite one example. Capua, in Campania, was the largest city in Italy except Rome, and it was the richest city on the peninsula, second only to Rome itself. In 216 B.C., following Hannibal's devastating defeat of the Romans at Cannae, Capua revolted against Rome and went over to Hannibal's side. But Hannibal had no spare troops with which to garrison cities that yielded to him, and this revealed a severe weakness in Hannibal's overall situation. His was an army of conquest, not an army of occupation. The Romans besieged the city and, in 211 B.C., after five years of infidelity toward Rome, Capua was doomed to fall, and its inhabitants recognized their fate.

Vibibus Virrius, a Capuan, who had been one of the main instigators of collusion with Hannibal, said to the governing body of Capua that he would never be chained and dragged through the streets of Rome, only to be bound to a stake, to be scourged and beheaded. He said all those who wished to yield to fate and avoid witnessing the destruction of the city should attend a banquet which he had prepared at his house. After they had eaten and drunk to their satisfaction, he said, the same cup would be passed to them that had been given to him. A toast containing poison would spare their bodies of torture, their minds of insult, their eyes the sight and their ears the sound of the wretched indignities that were sure to befall the conquered. There would be persons, prepared to place their lifeless bodies on a huge funeral pyre in the courtyard of his house. This, said Vibibus, was the honorable way to death.

Livy, the Roman historian, tells us that twenty-seven senators accompanied Vibibus to his house and dined with him. So far as they were able, they drowned all thought of impending doom in wine, and then drank the poison. With the banquet finished, they grasped each other's hands, and, with one final embrace, breathed their last before the gates of the city were opened to the Romans.

Vibibus was right in his estimation of the Roman desire for vengeance. Seventy collaborators who had been compromised in the decision to revolt against Rome were executed, along with other leaders. Three hundred nobles were condemned to chains.

After the executions had been ended by the decree of the Roman Senate, one of the Capuans, Jubellius Taurea—spelled with a J; I am advised that in that language and in those ancient times, there was no letter with a J sound in the alphabet. So, while it is spelled J-u-b-e-l-l-i-u-s, the letter J was pronounced as a Y—Jubellius Taurea approached the Roman consul, Fulvius, and cried out to him: "Since thou art so thirsty for our blood, why not strike me thyself that thou mayest boast of having killed a braver man than thou"?

Fulvius answered: "I should like well to do it but a decree of the Senate forbids."

Jubellius rejoined, "Well, then, I will show thee something that thou wouldst not have the courage to do," whereupon, he killed his wife, his children, and then himself. The people were sold into slavery, and Capua and its territory became part of the Roman domain.

Madam President, we have followed the expansion of Roman territory between 264 B.C. and 133 B.C., and noted that it left Rome in control of the Mediterranean. Rome organized new provinces in Africa, in Asia, in Hither Spain and Farther Spain; she extended her dominion over Macedonia and Greece, and restored her control over Cisalpine Gaul, which had been disturbed during the Hannibalic invasion. She also extended her dominion over Sicily, Sardinia, Corsica, the Balearic Islands and other islands in the western Mediterranean Sea. The growth in Roman territory had been phenomenal.

ROMAN SENATE IN FULL CONTROL

Also during this period, the Senate had increased its power and influence. Several facts account for the growth in the Senate's power. First of all, during the Second Punic War, the Senate had taken over the control of the government entirely. It took over the war, and emerged from the war more powerful

[95]

than ever. Second, unlike the consuls, who at the end of their one-year term were subject to having to answer to the Roman people for any mistakes they had made during their term of office, the Senate was a permanent organ of government, and senators held office for life.

The source of the Senate's power was its *auctoritas*, a concept which carried both religious and constitutional connotations. In practice, the term meant the prestige and esteem that the Senate possessed, based on custom and precedent and the outstanding qualities of the members. Only to the Senate belonged the dignity of an antique tradition, unbroken from the earliest beginnings of the Roman state. The Roman Senate had existed from the time of the kings, having been created by the legendary first king, Romulus. It had survived over two hundred years under the monarchy and had now continued through almost four hundred years under the republic. Constitutionally, *auctoritas* was the root of the power to ratify the laws of the popular assembly, approve the elections of magistrates, issue *senatus consulta* advising those magistrates, and control the public finances.

We have noted, time and time again, that before a bill or resolution could become law, it had to be approved by the Roman Senate. Therefore, there existed a check and balance between the popular assembly and the Senate. As in our own legislative process, a bill, before it can become law, must pass both houses and be exactly similar in every jot and tittle— every period, semicolon, colon, parenthesis, and number. Underlying the system requiring legislation to be approved by both bodies during the Roman republic, was the religious idea that a bill or resolution, to become law, had to be pleasing to the gods.

The Roman Senate, as I have stated time and again, had complete control of the finances. No moneys could be earmarked for war, no moneys could be earmarked for public works except by the Senate. A soldier could not receive his pay nor a victorious general his triumph unless money for the purpose had been provided by the Senate. The Senate's control over the finances and over military and foreign policy, and even over the courts, remained unchallenged until the time of Tiberius Gracchus in 133 B.C.

[96]

The Roman Senate often reduced the consuls and other magistrates to obedient executors of the Senate's will. Even the tribunes, formerly the champions and protectors of the people, had become the willing tools and accomplices of the Senate. Not even the powerful censors, except for the irascible and aggressive Cato, ventured to challenge its authority.

The handicaps that a new man, *novus homo*, had to overcome to gain one of the higher offices or a seat in the Senate were numerous and difficult. Only a rich man could stand the expenses of an election campaign and hold an office for which he was paid no salary. His chances of election were slim if he was opposed by a member of an old and illustrious family supported by numerous clans, powerful friends, and influential connections. Only men with exceptional ability and personality, like Cato, Marius, or Cicero, could burst the bars of exclusion. Such was the closed caste that ruled the Senate.

Marcus Tullius Cicero was convinced that the preservation of republican government depended upon maintaining the supremacy of the Senate. We will see more of Cicero in future days. His concept of the ideal state was one that was governed according to law. To the magistrates would be allotted executive power; to the Senate, authority; and to the people, liberty.

As we turn now to the final century of the republic, let us remember that the old Roman virtues—so much like the religious and family values and other virtues in American life that we have known since the beginning, and prior thereto, of our own republic—had guided the Roman people through six hundred years of wars and trials and triumphs, from the time when Rome was but a struggling, fledgling city on the Tiber to her present position as the foremost world power. The Roman virtues of honesty, frugality, adaptability to changing circumstances, abhorrence of bribery and corruption, respect for law, and the admirable balance of their government—I emphasize this—the admirable balance among the powers of the consuls, the Senate, and the popular Assembly, in a mixed government, still drew the admiration of Polybius as late as about 150 B.C.

POWERFUL TRANSFORMATION IN ECONOMIC AND SOCIAL LIFE

During this period, beginning with the expansion of Roman territory, and more particularly during the second century B.C., economic and social life throughout the peninsula underwent profound changes. Despite Rome's immense conquest of land, all too many people in Rome and throughout Italy suffered from poverty, want, privation, and famine.

Large plantation-type farms, cultivated by slave labor, began to replace the small family farms. Only the wealthy had the capital to introduce new kinds of crops and new breeds of livestock. The spread of the *latifundia*—large landed estates—caused thousands of peasants to lose their homesteads and drove increasing numbers of small farmers from the countryside to unemployment in the towns. There was a pressing need to reestablish a small peasantry on the land and to rid the cities of idle hands.

TIBERIUS GRACCHUS

At this time, there suddenly burst upon the stage of human history, Tiberius Sempronius Gracchus, the public-spirited son of one of Rome's most eminent aristocrats who was married to Cornelia, the daughter of Publius Cornelius Scipio Africanus Major. Many of us have heard the story of Cornelia, who married a Tiberius Gracchus, the father of the Tiberius Sempronius Gracchus of whom I now speak. Cornelia was the mother of twelve children. She lost all of her children except three—two sons, Tiberius and Gaius, and one daughter, Sempronia. One day, a neighbor came by to visit Cornelia and proudly displayed her jewelry. Haughtily turning to Cornelia, the woman asked, "Do you have any jewelry?" Cornelia, great Roman matron, mother of the Gracchi, turned to her two remaining sons, Tiberius and Gaius, and proudly said, "These are my jewels."

Tiberius Sempronius Gracchus was elected tribune for the year 133 B.C., and he saw, in the movement of small farmers away from the land and into the cities, a menace to the Roman state. He, therefore, introduced a law to deal with the problem of overpopulation in Rome and to reestablish the Italian peasantry on the land. His bill provided that the soldiers and the peasants were to be settled on the large landed estates

[98]

that had been captured by the republic in its many wars in Italy and leased to wealthy ranchers. Of course, his legislation ran into opposition. He sought to placate the rich landowners, but, in spite of his efforts, the legislation was vetoed by Marcus Octavius, who was also a tribune. Tiberius resorted to an unprecedented procedure. He introduced a motion to depose Marcus Octavius from his office of tribune. It was an illegal procedure, but it carried. Octavius was deposed. The land legislation then became law.

Tiberius and his brother Gaius and his father-in-law, Appius Claudius Pulchur, were elected as the three members of the land commission to enforce the land law. The Senate refused to appropriate moneys needed by the land commission to carry out its work, whereupon Tiberius proposed that the money be provided from property left to Rome by the bequest of King Attalus III of Pergamum shortly before his death. This was an unheard of thing. The Senate, from time immemorial, had exercised complete control over the treasury. But here, Tiberius was proposing to circumvent the Senate and obtain the money from a foreign source. This was a blow to the Senate and its traditional power over the public purse and foreign policy. Moreover, Tiberius announced his candidacy for reelection to the office of tribune, arousing fears of tyrannical power even among some of his previous supporters. Many senators violently opposed his reelection, and a mob led by Tiberius' cousin killed him and several of his followers and dumped their bodies into the Tiber. Tiberius' tribunate is said to have marked the introduction of murder into Roman politics and the beginning of the disintegration of the ruling oligarchy.

GAIUS GRACCHUS

Ten years later, in 123 B.C., Gaius Gracchus, younger brother of Tiberius, was elected tribune. He supported the agrarian policy of his dead brother Tiberius, but his aims were even more far reaching than the policies of Tiberius and made Gaius even more popular than Tiberius, so much more in fact that, in spite of custom and practice, he was reelected to the office of tribune for the year 122 B.C.

The changes that Gaius Gracchus brought about favored the business class, as well as the proletariat, and were clearly

[ 99 ]

designed to weaken the Senate. After laws meant to avenge his brother, he passed a program of radical reform, including agrarian laws reviving land distribution and laws regulating army service and providing free clothing to soldiers, as well as laws providing for public works throughout Italy—all these being calculated to relieve poverty and to gain the support of the plebeians. Is one thus reminded of populist overtures by today's politicians?

Gaius brought forth a series of measures seeking to undermine the existing aristocratic republican form of government. He proposed to give Roman citizenship to Latins and Latin status to other Italians. He also had laws passed to establish juries consisting of non-senators, or Equites, rather than senators or relatives of senators, and bringing about the transfer of control over the court system from the senatorial order and placing it in the hands of businessmen, who were henceforth referred to collectively as the Equestrian order. Today's devotees of affirmative action should take note!

Gaius secured the support of the poorer plebeians of the capital by the regular distribution of grain by the government to the poor at a below-market price, thus constituting a regular charge upon the treasury and accepting the welfare state doctrine of responsibility for the poor. The era of food stamps was yet afar off, and the recipients of this cheap grain did not receive it free of all cost but had to pay a nominal amount for it, and while Gaius cannot be charged with having established a grain dole, the door had been opened for enterprising politicians to solicit the votes of the people at the expense of the government. Does this remind us of politicians in our own time?

Gaius achieved enactment of a law affecting the collection of taxes in the new province of Asia by requiring that public contracts for collection of the Asian tithe on agricultural produce be awarded to preferred companies of *publicani*, thus affording lucrative profits to Roman businessmen. This legislation endeared Gaius Gracchus to the business interests and won their political support. He, therefore, announced his candidacy for reelection to a third term as tribune.

But primarily through the machinations of the Optimates, Gaius' influence had declined, and with it his political power,

[100]

and he was defeated in his bid for reelection. His enemies' final success prepared the way for his self-ordered execution by a friendly slave.

The Gracchi brothers were gifted and dedicated reformers, but they did not always choose the right course to achieve meaningful reforms. Aiming at the relief of poverty and the checking of senatorial control, they in fact created, in the Equestrians, a new exploiting class, not restrained—as was the senatorial order—by an ancient tradition of public service and the exercise of political responsibility. In their efforts to force enactment of their measures, they undermined the foundations of the Roman constitution and weakened the Senate's authority and prestige. The Roman Senate was also weakened by the newly emerging unity and collective political opposition of the business interests fostered by the Gracchan policies.

As we endure the assaults of modern Gracchans on the legislative branch and the Constitution's checks and balances, are we to conclude that history must always and inexorably repeat itself?

Viewing these kaleidoscopic changes and events, we have seen emerging in the final third of the second century B.C., two opposing political factions—the Optimates and the Populares.

The Optimates were made up of the nobility or aristocracy and included most of the senatorial order who were dedicated to the continuation of government by the few. They resisted any changes in the status quo that affected their political or economic interests, and they opposed the political and economic programs of the Populares, who sought to extend the freedom of voting, and to rally the poor to their support through liberalized grain laws and agrarian reform. The Optimates had the advantages of wealth, large clienteles locally and in the provinces, and control of the Senate and the government.

The Populares represented the discontented and reform-minded elements, who demanded change in the status quo. Although most of the Populares' leaders came from a minority faction in the senatorial order, they constituted a political organization that worked through the people rather than the Senate, and challenged the predominance of the ruling oligarchy

[101]

of the Optimates. The resultant struggle was a central feature of domestic politics after 133 B.C.

The danger for the future lay in the diminishing assertiveness of an enervated Senate and in the divisive struggle for power by the antagonistic political adversaries—the Optimates and the Populares.

The Senate was headed into a slow decline which would be followed, in time, by the decline of the republic. It would be a slow process, brought about by bloody civil wars, the overextension of the territorial administration of the Roman government, the growing influence of the military and the military leaders, the continuing erosion of the Senate's power and authority, and the gradual corrosion of old Roman virtues and the Roman character.

Finally, despite the adherence of many senators to the ideals of the Roman moral tradition, the corrupting influence of wealth, of a slave economy, and of power politics had shown itself in the destruction of Carthage, Corinth, and Numantia. The rifts in the fabric were appearing.

Having transformed itself into an exclusive and arbitrary oligarchy, the Senate exposed itself to the attacks of the Gracchi. Their efforts toward reform—and especially the ways they chose to bring about reform—weakened the Senate and set in motion a chain of inexorable events that occurred over the next one hundred years and resulted in the final collapse of the republic.

We shall pursue these developments following the observance of America's Independence Day.

I yield the floor.

*To be ignorant of what occurred before you were born is to remain always a child. For what is the worth of human life unless it is woven into the lives of our ancestors by the records of history?*

Marcus Tullius Cicero

ᏬᎧᏂ

*The principal office of history I take to be this: to prevent virtuous actions from being forgotten, and that evil words and deeds should fear an infamous reputation with posterity.*

Tacitus

ᏬᎧᏂ

*I shall be content if those shall pronounce my history useful who wish to be given a view of events as they really happened, and as they are very likely to repeat themselves.*

Thucydides

ᏬᎧᏂ

*What chiefly makes the study of history wholesome and profitable is this, that you behold the lessons of every kind of experience set forth as on a conspicuous monument; from these you may choose for yourself and for your own state what to imitate, from these mark for avoidance what is shameful in the conception and shameful in the result . . .*

Livy

*Lucius Cornelius Sulla*

*Gaius Marius*

# CHAPTER 9

# War, Revolution, and Turmoil

*July 13, 1993*

Mr. BYRD. Mr. President, this is the ninth in my series of weekly one-hour speeches on the Roman people and their constitutional system of divided powers. In my speech of the week preceding the July 4 holiday, I spoke of the remarkable economic and social changes that had occurred in Rome and throughout Italy during the period of Rome's phenomenal territorial expansion in the third and second centuries B.C. I noted that there had been an emergence of two political factions: the Optimates, who represented the senatorial oligarchy and other aristocrats; and the Populares, or the people's party, who represented the proletariat and those elements that were discontented with the existing social order and who demanded certain reforms. I also observed the growing rivalry between the Senate and the Equestrian order. The roots of the Equestrian order went back to the days of early Rome, to the equites who composed the cavalry of the Roman armies.

We noted the rapid growth in the *latifundia*, the large plantation-type farms that spread throughout Italy and resulted in the diminishing number of small family farms from which had come the stalwart citizen soldiery during the centuries of the regal period and the early and the middle republic. We noted also the growing slave economy, and the serious problem of unemployment in the cities that resulted from the flight of the peasants from the land they had tilled for generations.

Tiberius Gracchus, who was a tribune in 133 B.C., had been traveling through Etruria when he noticed the dearth of inhabitants. He noted that the soil was tilled and the flocks were tended by slaves. And he wondered how the great Roman republic could continue to be independent and continue in its leadership if the vanishing peasantry were supplanted by slaves from foreign countries. In those days, in order to be a soldier one was required to have property. This concerned Tiberius and he saw, in the diminishing numbers of sturdy peasant stock, the future decline of the Roman legions.

I am reminded that Tiberius' concerns were echoed by Oliver Goldsmith in "The Deserted Village," who picked up the theme that had so disturbed Tiberius Gracchus:

> Ill fares the land, to hastening ills a prey,
> Where wealth accumulates, and men decay;
> Princes and lords may flourish, or may fade;
> A breath can make them, as a breath has made;
> But a bold peasantry, their country's pride,
> When once destroyed, can never be supplied.

Mr. President, we see in this, another parallel between the history of the Romans and the history of our own country as we have experienced the shift away from the small family farms to the large corporate farms, and the movement away from what was once a predominantly rural population in this country to huge, sprawling urban communities and megalopolises with their problems of poverty, disease, unemployment, crime, declining family values, and eroding religious values.

It was to these same problems, therefore, that Tiberius Gracchus, in 133 B.C., sought to address legislation which the Senate oligarchy violently opposed. His efforts toward reform cost him his life at the hands of a mob made up of slaves and clients of senators and other aristocrats.

I have mentioned the word "client" heretofore during this series of speeches, and I should digress momentarily to explain the meaning of the term when used in this context. In early Rome, it was customary for poorer citizens to attach themselves to a rich or influential citizen in return for his financial or legal assistance, and he thus became their patron. They became his clients. In return for his financial assistance and other types of aid, they gave to him their political support and their help in his private life. Obviously, it was a matter of great prestige

[ 106 ]

for the patron to appear in public surrounded by a large delegation of these respectful clients. They not only owed him their
political support and private help, but they also owed him
their respect, and they showed this by greeting him in the
morning and by accompanying him about the city.

Also, in those early times when enemy peoples were conquered or when an enemy city was captured, the conquered
peoples were sold as slaves. It was the right of any owner
of a slave to manumit that slave whenever and however he
pleased, and when the owner manumitted a slave, the freedman
then became his client and the former owner became the patron.
The law recognized this relationship. It had legal sanction.
For example, the patron and his client were not allowed to
give testimony against one another.

### The Fall of Gaius Gracchus

In 123 B.C., Gaius Gracchus, the younger brother of Tiberius,
was elected tribune—following the death of his brother by
a decade. In 122 B.C., Gaius was reelected tribune, contrary
to the established practice which precluded one's election to
the same office unless ten years had passed.

Gaius carried forward the agrarian policies of his dead
brother, but his designs went even further. Several of his laws
were clearly intended to strengthen the Equestrians and dilute
the powers of the Senate as, for example, his law changing
the composition of juries so as to exclude senators from sitting
on juries and to allow the replacement of senators as jurors
by Equestrians. That he fully recognized the significance and
the implications of this law was shown by his remark to someone that, even if he should die, he would leave it—meaning
the law—as a sword thrust into the side of the Senate.

Gaius also sought, like his brother before him, to reestablish
an Italian peasantry on the land as a means of bringing new
strength to the Roman armies, while, at the same time, ridding
the cities of idle hands.

Gaius was not successful in his effort to be elected tribune
for a third time. When he was no longer tribune, the consul,
Lucius Opimius, summoned Gaius to appear before the Senate
to answer questions concerning the actions that he, Gaius, had
taken during his two terms as tribune. Paterculus, the historian,

who lived between the years 19 B.C. and 30 A.D., writes that Gaius was determined not to be arrested and not to appear before the Roman Senate, and that, in his flight, at the point of time when he was about to be apprehended by the emissaries of Opimius, he offered his neck to the sword of his friendly slave, Euporus. The body of Gaius, like the body of Tiberius a decade before him, was unceremoniously cast into the Tiber, that he would not enjoy the quiet repose of the grave. Many of his followers were also executed.

The Senate had suffered a great loss to its prestige and its authority, and even though the Gracchan threat had been eliminated, the Senate owed its victory to violence. This afforded a precedent which might be turned against the Senate itself. Moreover, the alliance of the Equestrians and the urban proletariat had proved to be stronger than the Senate, and this, too, was a lesson that was not lost on future leaders ambitious for power.

### THE JUGURTHINE WAR

While at Rome the interest had been centered upon the struggle between the Gracchans and the Senate, Roman armies had been busy fighting wars in the defense of Roman territory, as a result of which, in 121 B.C., the Romans became masters of southern Gaul, from the Alps to the Pyrenees. In 112 B.C., Rome became involved in a serious conflict in North Africa. Her involvement revealed to the world the corruption of the ruling class in Rome. The occasion was the death, in 118 B.C., of Micipsa, successor to Masinissa, king of Numidia and loyal ally of Rome. Micipsa had bequeathed his kingdom to his two sons, Adherbal and Hiempsal, and to a nephew, Jugurtha, whom he had adopted several years before. When the two brothers as joint heirs challenged the bequest after Micipsa's death, Jugurtha had Hiempsal murdered and attacked Adherbal, who escaped to Rome and appealed for aid. The actions and motivations of the Roman Senate in the imbroglio that subsequently ensued are puzzling.

A commission headed by Lucius Opimius divided Numidia, giving the western and richer half to Jugurtha and the poorer half to Adherbal. Jugurtha, however, had no intention of ruling only half the country. In 112 B.C., he again attacked Adherbal, besieged him in the capital city of Cirta, and killed him. Many Italian businessmen died in the sack of the city which they had fought to defend, and a wave of anger and agitation for war swept over Rome. The Roman consul, Lucius Calpurnius Bestia, invaded Numidia but soon gave Jugurtha an easy peace under circumstances that suggested the use of bribes by Jugurtha. There was widespread discontent at this in Rome, where suspicions among the Equestrians led to demands for an investigation, and Jugurtha was summoned to appear before the Senate for questioning.

Jugurtha, according to the historian Sallust, had been told by friends that "everything at Rome had its price." Jugurtha, therefore, loaded with bribes for senators, arrived in Rome.

Sallust writes that there was in Rome at the time a Numidian called Massiva, a grandson of Masinissa, who was persuaded by a former consul to claim the Numidian throne. When Massiva started intriguing to achieve his purpose, Jugurtha, who had gotten wind of the matter, secured the help of a devoted and intimate attendant in procuring the assassination of the rival claimant. Much indignation toward Jugurtha was aroused as a result of the murder, but he was successful in buying the intervention of two Roman tribunes, who voted against the taking of any testimony from him. Yet, his friends in the Senate dared protect him no longer, and he was ordered to leave Italy.

### GAIUS MARIUS

The war was reopened, and a battle was fought in which the Roman army was defeated and forced to pass under the yoke, a matter of great humiliation, and released only after its commander had conceded to an alliance between Jugurtha and Rome. Treachery and bribery had played a part in this disgraceful episode. The Roman Senate rejected the terms of the agreement, and a new consul, Quintus Caecilius Metellus, surnamed Numidicus, took command. One of his staff officers was a man named Gaius Marius. Gaius Marius was an ambitious and able officer, and he implored Metellus that he, Marius, be allowed to go to Rome and stand for the office of consul. Metellus' reaction was one that insulted Marius, and from that time on, he had a bitter feeling toward Metellus and

[109]

intrigued against him. Finally, however, Metellus agreed to let Marius go to Rome to stand for consul.

In 107 B.C., Marius was elected consul, and the Populares secured the passage of a law by the Tribal Assembly transferring the command in Numidia from Metellus to Marius. Take note: the Senate yielded in this encroachment by the Populares on its traditional rights. Marius pursued the battle in North Africa with energy, enthusiasm, and effectiveness. His quaestor, or quartermaster, was Lucius Cornelius Sulla, who was destined to become a bitter rival.

Marius pressed the war with great vigor and won hard-fought victories over Jugurtha and his father-in-law Bocchus, king of Mauretania. Sulla, in due time, was successful in capturing Jugurtha, at great risk to his own life. He captured Jugurtha through the treachery of Bocchus, whose betrayal of his son-in-law brought an end to the war. Jugurtha was taken to Rome where he was executed after gracing the triumph of Marius in 105 B.C.

The war had seriously undermined the credibility of the Roman Senate, which had already suffered from the reforms directed against it during the years when it was under attack at the hands of the Gracchi.

The venality of senators in dealing with the unscrupulous Jugurtha, and the transfer of the command in Numidia from Metellus to Marius by the Populares, had damaged the Senate's prestige and authority. The Equestrians and the city proletariat had shown that, by acting together, they could dictate foreign policy. Also emerging from the war was a military leader— Gaius Marius—who possessed the skills to unite these forces in the future.

Marius was again elected consul in 104 B.C., the Roman people disregarding the required legal interval of ten years, and he was given the command against the northern barbarians in Gaul. He set to work immediately in reorganizing and strengthening the Roman army. He instituted improvements in training and in weapons and equipment, established greater efficiency in the organization of his forces, and developed new and innovative tactics, thus providing the legions with greater mobility and power than before.

Plutarch writes that Marius trained his soldiers to labour while on the road, accustoming them to long and tedious marches, and compelling every man to carry his own baggage and provide his own victuals. From that time afterwards, "laborius people, who executed readily and without murmuring" whatever they were ordered to do, were called "Marius's mules."

Marius, a man of sterness and discipline and austerity of behavior, was fierce and intractable when in authority, and was possessed of great fortitude in enduring pain. Plutarch cites an instance of extraordinary proof of this in his bearing a surgical operation. Having both his legs full of wens, Marius determined to put himself in the hands of a surgeon. He would not be bound but stretched out one of his legs to the knife, and, without motion or groan, bore the inexpressible pain of the operation in silence and with a settled countenance. But when the surgeon was going to begin with the other leg, Plutarch relates that Marius would not permit him to do so, saying, "I see the cure is not worth the pain."

Whereas the ownership of property had long been a requirement for entry into military service, Marius opened the door of recruitment to all, enrolling men who owned no property and were previously exempt. In accepting such troops, he remedied the long-standing manpower shortage and opened up a career for the employment of thousands of landless and jobless citizens. By this innovation, Marius created a new type of client army, bound to its commander as its patron. A successful Roman general, rather than the Roman state, would henceforth command the loyalties of the Roman legions. Marius' genius made possible, for the first time, the creation of large standing armies, both at home and in the provinces.

Since the threat from the northern barbarians continued, Marius was reelected consul for the years 103, 102, and 101 B.C. In his fifth term as consul in 101 B.C., Marius was victorious over the Cimbri and the Teutones, and Rome was thereby saved from a repetition of the Gallic invasion of the fourth century B.C.

A coalition among three men—Lucius Appuleius Saturninus and Gaius Servilius Glaucia and Marius—resulted in a sixth term as consul for Marius, in the year 100 B.C., the year in which Julius Caesar, a nephew of Marius by marriage, was born. It also resulted in Saturninus' reelection to the office of tribune for a second term, and a praetorship for Glaucia. Glaucia and Saturninus became candidates for the following year, 99 B.C., but Glaucia had a rival candidate murdered, which provoked violent disorders. The Senate adopted a decree calling on Marius to restore order. Marius forced the surrender of Glaucia and Saturninus and placed them in a building for safe keeping, but their enemies tore off the roof of the building and stoned them, as a result of which Marius was forced to go into seclusion for several years.

The Senate had gained while the Populares had suffered in the public's esteem. The Optimates sought to put a halt to democratic reform legislation by prohibiting the inclusion of extraneous matter in bills and by making omnibus bills illegal. They also required rigid enforcement of a rule which provided for a lapse of three days between the reporting of, and voting on, a bill—much like our own two-day rule.

I see my friend from Mississippi, Mr. Cochran, smiling; I also see a smile on my friend's face from Alaska, Mr. Stevens; they know what I am about to say. Here, 2,092 years ago, in the Roman Senate, was a type of Byrd Rule—a precursor to that under which the U.S. Senate operates—dealing with unrelated and extraneous matter. Perhaps an awareness of this rule of parliamentary procedure in ancient Rome will help the members of the United States Senate and the House of Representatives to better appreciate and understand the importance and significance of the Byrd Rule in our own Senate.

## NON-ROMAN ITALIANS: CIVIL WARS

In 91 B.C., a Roman tribune, Livius Drusus, promised non-Roman Italians that he would bring forth legislation to give them Roman citizenship. The Senate and the Equestrians were very much opposed to this, and Drusus, learning of a plot against his life, removed himself to the atrium of his house, where he transacted the public's business. It was poorly lighted, and one evening, when he was sending a crowd away, he suddenly exclaimed that he was wounded, and fell down while uttering the words. A shoemaker's knife was found thrust into his back.

[112]

When the Italians heard of the murder of Drusus, they considered it no longer tolerable for those who were laboring for their political advancement to suffer such outrages and, as they saw no other means of acquiring citizenship, they decided to join in a revolt against the Romans and to make war against them. They, therefore, sent envoys secretly to one another, formed a league, and exchanged hostages as a pledge of good faith. They also sent ambassadors to Rome to complain that, although they had helped Rome to fight its wars of conquest, the Romans had not been willing to admit the Italians to citizenship. The Roman Senate sternly rejected their pleas.

Appianus—or Appian, as he is commonly known—states in his history of the civil wars that when the revolt broke out, all the neighboring peoples declared war at the same time. Thus, in the year 90 B.C., the Social War began. It is sometimes referred to as the Marsic War, sometimes as the Italic War, and sometimes as the War against the Allies. The non-Roman Italians had forces amounting to about 100,000 foot soldiers and horsemen, aside from the soldiers that remained as guards in each town. The Romans sent an equal force against them, composed of the legions and the Italian peoples who were still in alliance with Rome. The Romans were led by the two consuls, Sextus Julius Caesar and Publius Rutilius Lupus. Serving with them as lieutenant generals were such renowned men as Gaius Marius, Lucius Cornelius Sulla, Gaius Perpenna, Publius Licinius Crassus, Gnaeus Pompeius Strabo, the father of Pompey and under whom both Pompey and Cicero served during the Social War. The non-Roman armies had several very able generals, as well, to lead their united forces.

The consul Rutilius Lupus lost his life in the war, as did tens of thousands of others on both sides. The body of Rutilius, along with the bodies of many others, was brought to Rome for burial. Their corpses made a piteous spectacle. The Roman Senate decreed that from that time, those who were killed in the war should be buried where they fell, lest the spectacle deter others from entering the army.

Another consul, Cato Porcius, subsequently was killed. The Romans finally decided to bring an end to this terrible war, which was costing them so heavily in treasure and in blood. They, therefore, conceded the issues at stake. All Italy was now united, and all of the peoples south of the Po River received Roman citizenship. By promising Roman citizenship to all those who had not yet revolted or who would lay down their arms, the Roman Senate belatedly acknowledged the folly of its policy opposing Drusus.

## SULLA

The revolt had brought Marius out of exile. The Senate had already appointed Lucius Cornelius Sulla (Sylla) to the command in Asia Minor against the able and ambitious king of Pontus, Mithridates VI, Eupator. However, with the aid of a demagogic tribune, Publius Sulpicius Rufus, the command in Asia Minor was transferred by law to Marius, whereupon Sulla marched his army back to Rome. Marius and Rufus hastily collected troops to fight a pitched battle of Romans against Romans in and around the city itself. Appian writes: "Now for the first time, an army of her own citizens invaded Rome as a hostile country. From this time, all civil dissensions were decided only by the arbitrament of arms."

Sulla was victorious. Marius barely escaped with his life to Mauretania. Sulpicius Rufus was killed and his head severed from his body and nailed to the rostrum in the Forum. We are told that Sulpicius had been betrayed by a slave, and that Sulla rewarded the slave for his services by freeing him, and then having him executed for his treachery.

Sulla hastily tried to reorganize the Roman government by strengthening the Roman Senate and reviving the army assembly, the Comitia Centuriata, and by using it to replace the Tribal Assembly, the Comitia Tributa. Leaving two consuls, Lucius Cornelius Cinna and Gnaeus Octavius, both of whom were sworn to support the new constitution, Sulla hurried off to fight Mithridates in Asia Minor. He had not been gone long before Cinna impeached Sulla and proposed the recall of Marius. The Senate deposed Cinna. He was driven from the city by the other consul, Gnaeus Octavius.

Cinna fled to raise an army, to return and besiege Rome. Marius also returned, and the two of them overcame all resistance, again capturing Rome with a Roman army. With a cruelty beyond belief, they hunted down their opponents. Octavius

[114]

and leading senators and equites were brutally slain. Appian writes:

> They killed remorselessly. All the heads of Senators were exposed in front of the rostrum. All the friends of Sulla were put to death. His home was razed to the ground, his property confiscated, and himself voted a public enemy. A search was made for his wife and children, but they escaped.

Marius died early in 86 B.C., soon after beginning his seventh term as consul. Cinna was left to lord it over Rome, where he was supreme as consul for that year and for the succeeding two years. Meanwhile, in Asia Minor, Sulla was victorious. He had slain thousands and collected a vast treasury. He now prepared to return with a well-equipped, seasoned army to exact the terrible revenge which he had been planning in cold blood. Cinna was under no illusions as to the fate that awaited him. He started with an army to sail to Macedonia to intercept Sulla. But Cinna was assassinated by his own soldiers in a mutiny at Brundisium, and the fleet did not sail. The followers of Marius and Cinna, nevertheless, would not yield in Italy without a struggle.

Sulla landed in Italy in 83 B.C., and, at the Colline Gate, destroyed an opposing army, massacring to the man the Samnites who had joined it. With a ruthless barbarity, he pursued all those whom he considered to be his enemies, putting up proscription lists of their names and declaring rewards for those who murdered them or who informed against them. Paterculus, the historian, says that Sulla "was the first to set the precedent for proscription." Plutarch says, "Husbands were dispatched in the bosoms of their wives and sons in those of their mothers." The innocent rich were included in the proscription lists in order that their property might be confiscated. All of Italy was in terror of Sulla's name. After a while, the proscriptions ceased and Sulla went about the business of reorganizing the government.

Sulla was named dictator in 82 B.C. He had brought about the appointment of an interrex who, under a special law, then appointed Sulla as dictator for an indeterminate term. This meant that Sulla had all the powers of consuls and tribunes and censors, the combined powers of all the magistrates. Whereas the old practice had allowed the appointment of a dictator for a limited term of no more than six months, this new law made possible an open-ended appointment. Sulla, by virtue of this unlimited term and the scope of his powers, became the most powerful person in Roman history up to that time. He had unprecedented autocratic authority.

### SENATE STRENGTHENED AND CORRUPTED

Sulla was now the complete and absolute master of Italy. He reshaped the Roman government to suit his own conservative ideas. He made the Roman Senate the most powerful body in the state, weakened the powers of the tribunes, subjected all magistrates to strict accountability, and deprived the Equestrians of the privilege, granted to them by Gaius Gracchus, of sitting as judges in their own cause. Sulla also sought to improve the caliber of men sent to govern the republic's growing empire. He tightened up the whole machinery of government, and settled thousands of his veterans on land throughout Italy that had been confiscated from the vast numbers who had perished or been proscribed in the frightful slaughter he had let loose. When Sulla voluntarily retired in the year 79 B.C., he depended upon his aristocratic friends not to allow any infraction of the revised form of senatorial government that he had created. He died the following year, 78 B.C., probably from colon cancer.

Mr. President, as we look back now, we see momentous changes that have taken place. Elderly Romans who were boys in the days prior to Tiberius Gracchus had seen their world overturned. Young Romans like Pompey and Cicero, who were 28 years of age, and Julius Caesar, who was 21, when Sulla retired, had lived through unspeakable horrors that were utterly alien to the traditional, idealized notions that they had held about their country. Rome was still a republic, but it was far different from the republic that had already been in existence 350 years when it attracted the admiration of the historian Polybius in the middle of the second century B.C. The army was no longer made up of the tough rural farmers, many of whom had come from the most mountainous areas of the peninsula. Marius, in creating a professional army, had created

[116]

a new base of power for ambitious men to exploit and use as an instrument of despotic authority.

And what of the Roman Senate? In the old heroic days, the Senate had been the most powerful body in the state. It had held supreme power because of the respect given to its wise, courageous, and incorruptible leadership. But the power that Sulla conferred upon the Senate—he had increased the number of senators to six hundred during his dictatorship—the power that Sulla conferred on Roman senators made them neither wise nor courageous. As to the incorruptibility of the Senate—which Cineas in 280 B.C., had compared to "a council of many kings,"—its sad decline was pregnant in the prescient words uttered by Jugurtha 170 years later at the time he was ordered to leave Italy. After passing through the gates of Rome, it is said that he looked back at the city several times in silence. Suddenly he exclaimed, "Yonder is a city put up for sale, and its days are numbered if it finds a buyer."

Mr. President, the republic's days were numbered.

I yield the floor.

*Catiline Confronted in the Senate by Cicero*

# CHAPTER 10

# Death Throes of the Roman Republic

*July 21, 1993*

Mr. BYRD. Mr. President, this is the tenth in my series of speeches on the Roman republic and its constitutional system of mixed government. Last week, I spoke of the proscriptions of Sulla. From Asia, Sulla had announced to the Senate his victories and his treaty with Mithridates, and had made no mention of personal grievances or revenge. However, after he had left Ephesus and crossed over to Greece and had reached the shore of the Adriatic, his tone changed. He sent a second message to the Senate, recapitulating the services that he had rendered to his country and the rewards that he had received for those services: his property confiscated, his friends assassinated, and himself voted a public enemy. He was now coming, he said, in order that his enemies and the enemies of the republic should receive the punishment due for their crimes.

## PROSCRIPTIONS OF SULLA

Sulla's return to Rome was a sanguinary one. The battle at the Colline Gate had been desperate and bloody, and the fighting had lasted all day long and throughout the entire night. The Samnite army, whose lines of retreat had been cut, was destroyed. And the battlefield, heaped with corpses, had grudgingly yielded up the victory to Sulla and his veterans.

On the day after the battle, Sulla was haranguing the Senate at the very moment that six thousand Samnite and Lucanian prisoners were perishing under the sword. Suddenly, the death cries were heard. Senators were struck with astonishment. But Sulla, with a firm and unaltered countenance, continued his discourse and bade the senators to pay attention to what he

[119]

was saying, for the noise, he said, was coming only from some malefactors whom he had ordered to be chastised.

The bloody battle at the Colline Gate had ended all effective resistance in Italy. Now, a reign of terror began, and Sulla posted proscription lists of intended victims who were to be hunted down like animals, murdered, and a price set upon their heads.

Many victims had already perished, when Gaius Metellus ventured to rise in the Senate and question Sulla as to when "this vengeance might be expected to stop." Sulla answered that he did not know. "Then," implored Metellus, "let us know whom thou intendest to destroy." Sulla said that he would do it. Plutarch tells us that Sulla then immediately posted a list of the names of eighty citizens. On the following day, he proscribed 220 more. And on the third day, as many more. Sulla then announced that he had completed the lists of all those names he remembered, and that those whose names he had forgotten—as he later would remember the names—they "must enter some future proscription list."

Even the dead were not spared of Sulla's vengeance. The corpse of Marius, the conqueror of the Cimbri and the Teutones, was exhumed and decapitated and given up to insults, and then cast contemptuously into the Anio—the Anienus River—that the repose of the grave might be denied him.

From the proscriptions the Equestrians had suffered especially. Appian, the historian, tells us that 15 ex-consuls, 90 senators, and 2,600 knights—or Equestrians—had already been the victims of the proscriptions. But proscription did not end with the death of the victims. It also struck at their posterity to the third generation. Not only were the sons and grandsons denied any paternal inheritance, but they also were declared unworthy ever to fill any public office.

Sulla, before he had left Asia, had requested of his friends in the Senate that a law be passed permitting the appointment of a dictator for an unlimited term; it was entirely without precedent. The two consuls being dead, Sulla then had himself appointed by an interrex, Valerius Flaccus, to the office of dictator for an unlimited term. The appointment carried with it all of the powers of all of the magistrates. Sulla was appointed

[120]

to an unlimited term in late 82 B.C., for the purpose of enacting legislation and reconstituting the government.

Sulla increased the number of senators from three hundred—the figure at which it had stood for over four hundred years—to six hundred. He appointed many of his own supporters, especially from among the Equestrians. As a consequence, the appointees to the Senate were beholden to Sulla. He then took away the traditional rights of the tribunes. They no longer had the right to introduce legislation. And he revised the composition of juries to again exclude Equestrians, but to include senators.

Sulla, indubitably, did not aim at a dictatorship for life. After he had restored "republican" government under senatorial control, he abdicated his power in stages, resigning from the dictatorship at the end of 81 B.C., being consul in 80, and becoming a private citizen without office in 79 B.C., retiring to his Campanian estate. Sulla died the next year at the age of 60. He composed his own epitaph: "No friend ever did me so much good, or enemy, so much harm, but I repaid him with interest."

### SUPINE AND INDOLENT SENATE

After Sulla's death in 78 B.C., Roman history moved around the names of a small group of eminent men whose ambitions and rivalries were given free rein by the progressive decline of the already supine and increasingly feeble authority wielded by an indolent Senate. The generation of Marius and Sulla had seen the organization and effective use of a professional army as the basis of political power in the state and in the provinces.

Mr. President, time precludes me from mention of the several wars being waged in this period, with the exception of certain conflicts involving the most eminent men.

Mithridates VI Eupator the Great, king of Pontus, had made peace with Sulla in 85 B.C. Realizing that Sulla made peace only to accommodate his own early return to Italy, where he had some scores to settle with Cinna and Carbo, Mithridates prepared for a renewal of the struggle with Rome. He defended himself against attack in 83 B.C. and in 82 B.C. by the Roman

General Lucius Licinius Murena. But, again, Sulla brought about a cessation of the hostilities.

In 75 B.C., the king of Bithynia, Nicomedes III, died after bequeathing to Rome his kingdom. After the Senate had accepted the kingdom and made it into a new province, Mithridates disputed its possession and invaded Bithynia in early 74 B.C., where he was confronted with the Roman consul Marcus Aurelius Cotta, whom he defeated. In this third Mithridatic war, a Roman general by the name of Lucius Licinius Lucullus defeated Mithridates on land and on sea, recovered Bithynia and invaded Pontus, Mithridates' kingdom, thus forcing Mithridates to take refuge with his son-in-law, Tigranes, the king of Armenia. For the next two years, Lucullus completed the subjugation of Pontus, but he could not end the war as long as Mithridates was at large. He, therefore, demanded the surrender of Mithridates by Tigranes, whose refusal of the demand resulted in an invasion of Armenia by Lucullus.

Lucullus defeated Tigranes and tried to completely subjugate Armenia, but he was prevented from doing so because of the mutinous conduct of his own troops, who were displeased because Lucullus protected the subject peoples from their excesses and, also, because Lucullus enforced strict discipline upon his troops. We can see why he had won these many battles. He enforced discipline among his troops, but they did not like it. He was thus forced to remain inactive, and finally, through the machinations of his enemies in Rome, Lucullus was relieved of his command in 66 B.C.

While Lucullus had been pursuing Mithridates in Asia Minor, Gnaeus Pompeius Magnus—Pompey the Great—was fighting Quintus Sertorius in Spain. As if two wars were not enough, a serious slave insurrection occurred in Italy. In 73 B.C., Spartacus, a Roman slave and gladiator from Thrace, broke out of the gladiatorial school at Capua with seventy of his fellow gladiators. He quickly collected more than ten thousand adherents and took refuge on Mount Vesuvius. He then vanquished the Roman forces that were sent against him under Varinius Glaber and Publius Valerius, after which his army swelled to a number of seventy thousand and eventually reached as many as 120,000.

[122]

Rome then sent both consuls against Spartacus and, after defeating their legions, he sacrificed three hundred Roman prisoners. This formidable war—although it had been ridiculed in the beginning as being nothing more than a raid, with much plundering and robbing—was now going into its third year.

### CRASSUS AND POMPEY

Marcus Licinius Crassus was elected praetor. His surname was "Dives." Remember the name in the Bible—Dives? Crassus was called "Dives" because of his great wealth. He advanced against Spartacus with six new legions. After arriving at his destination, he received two additional legions that had been defeated under the previous consuls. Crassus immediately decimated these two legions, killing every tenth man, as punishment for their bad performance in the battles they had lost against Spartacus.

Upon Crassus' demonstrating to his army that they had more to fear from him than from the enemy, he overcame ten thousand Spartacans and then advanced boldly against Spartacus himself, vanquished him in a brilliant engagement, and pursued his fleeing forces to the sea, where they attempted to pass over to Sicily. In a pitched battle that was long and bloody, Spartacus, with a great mass of his followers, was surrounded by the forces of Crassus and slain. Crassus had won a great victory over the slave rebels.

Meanwhile, in Spain, Marcus Veiento Perperna, having treacherously assassinated Sertorius, and having taken over his command, himself was disastrously defeated. He was taken prisoner and executed by Pompey, thus bringing an end to the war in Spain in the year 71 B.C., the same year in which Crassus had triumphed in the slave war.

Both Pompey and Crassus, flushed now by their victories— respectively, in Spain and in Italy—demanded triumphs, and also requested permission to stand as candidates for the consulship. Crassus was eligible, but Pompey was still under the age limit. He also did not qualify because he had not previously held the offices of quaestor and praetor.

Both Pompey and Crassus, however, having maintained their men under arms, the Senate was overawed and yielded, giving both men their triumphs, and approving the passage of a law exempting Pompey from the legal requirements of his candidacy. Both Pompey and Crassus then put aside their personal rivalries and supported each other to the fullest for the consulship. They were both elected. They immediately went to work and overturned the Sullan constitution, restoring to the tribunes their traditional rights, including the power of the veto. They revised the senatorial lists to include their own favorites, and also revised the composition of the juries, this time to provide that Equestrians as well as senators could sit thereon.

Both Pompey and Crassus had declined appointments in the provinces following their term as consul because there were no provinces available that offered them the opportunity to augment their military or political reputations. Subsequently, however, Pompey was given such opportunity by virtue of the ravages of the Cilician pirates, whose depredations upon shipping had interrupted the importation into Rome of grain, bringing on the serious threat of a famine and requiring decisive measures.

In 67 B.C., a Roman tribune by the name of Aulus Gabinius introduced legislation appointing a single commander of consular rank, with authority over the whole sea within the Pillars of Hercules and all Roman territory to a distance of fifty miles inland, the appointment—with Imperium—to last for three years. The Senate bitterly resisted this legislation, but it was enacted with the support of Marcus Tullius Cicero and that of a rising young noble named Gaius Julius Caesar. The opinion of the people was such that the Senate had to appoint Pompey.

Pompey immediately set to work energetically and systematically, and in forty days had swept the pirates from the western Mediterranean, and in forty-nine more had cornered them in Cilicia and forced the surrender of their strongholds. Thus, within three months, Pompey had brought to a triumphant conclusion the pirate war, but he still had thirty-three months to run with respect to his appointment with Imperium. He was eager to gather fresh laurels. The opportunity was not wanting, if we recall that the conclusion of the pirate war coincided with the check of Roman arms in Pontus and Armenia that had been brought about by the mutinous conduct of Lucullus' soldiers and the machinations of Lucullus' enemies in Rome.

[124]

Pompey sought Lucullus' command. Here was another opportunity for military glory. The Senate strongly opposed any extension of Pompey's authority. But with Cicero's support, again, legislation was enacted and Pompey received Lucullus' command, and he departed to carry out his new duties.

Tigranes came to terms with Pompey in 66 B.C. Mithridates in 63 B.C., was beset by a mutiny led by his own son, Pharnaces II, and trapped in his own citadel at Pantacapaeum, which was located in the Crimea at the site of present-day Kerch on the strait connecting the Sea of Azov with the Black Sea.

Mithridates attempted to commit suicide with poison, but he had been taking small doses of poison for several years and was, therefore, immune to poison. Therefore, he had himself put to death by a mercenary. With the death of Mithridates, the several Mithridatic wars came to an end.

Pompey had conquered a vast territory and had created a continuous belt of Roman provinces along the coasts of the Black Sea and the Caspian Sea and extending as far south as Syria and Judea. He then prepared, in 62 B.C., for a triumphal return with his victorious troops to Italy.

### THE CONSPIRACY OF CATILINE

Now, Mr. President, let us go back two years and see what was happening in Italy while Pompey was fighting in Asia Minor with Mithridates and Tigranes. In 64 B.C., three men ran as candidates for the consulship: Lucius Sergius Catilina, or Catiline; Gaius Antonius; and Marcus Tullius Cicero. Antonius and Cicero were elected. In 63 B.C., the consular elections for the next year were held and, again, Catiline ran and was again defeated, he being bitterly opposed by Cicero and the business interests and most senators, because they distrusted his motives.

Catiline was not a man to take two defeats easily. He was a vindictive man and of a rebellious nature. Therefore, while Gaius Manlius, an associate of his, was collecting a large force of men under arms in Etruria, Catiline, with contention and malice, formed a conspiracy in Rome against the government. The plan was to assassinate Cicero, create acts of arson throughout the city, and occupy strategic points with armed men who would take over the government.

[ 125 ]

Gaius Sallustius Crispus, a Roman historian who lived during the years 86 B.C. to 34 B.C., was a contemporary of this event. And he writes that among the conspirators was one Quintus Curtius, whom the censor had expelled from the Senate for bad conduct. Curtius had a lady friend whose name was Fulvia, and when he found himself less in favor with her because lack of means compelled him to be less lavish with his gifts, he suddenly began to talk big and promise her the Earth, the next moment threatening to stab her unless she complied with his demands. This high and mighty tone was so unlike his normal manner that Fulvia insisted upon an explanation. Upon discovering that there was a conspiracy, she decided that such a dangerous threat to Rome should not be concealed. The facts, therefore, were communicated to Cicero.

Cicero developed enough evidence to induce the Senate to adopt a decree empowering him to take all necessary measures to save the state. This was a *senatus consultum ultimum*, a declaration of a state of emergency. He then proceeded to have five of the leading accomplices of Catiline arrested. Instead of leaving the matter to the regular courts, Cicero promptly convened the Senate to decide the fate of the five prisoners. The Senate, after a very strong speech by Marcus Porcius Cato Uticensis the Younger, decreed that the conspirators be executed.

Cicero, believing it best not to wait until nightfall, lest an attempt be made by the conspirators during the interval, immediately conducted the condemned men to a chamber within the prison, which was about twelve feet below the ground and enclosed in walls of stone. Along with Publius Cornelius Lentulus Sura and Gaius Cornelius Cethegus, both of whom were senators, Gabinius and Statilius and Caeparius met death at the hands of the executioner on December 5, 63 B.C.

Catiline now realized that it would be futile to march on Rome, and he attempted to escape with his army into Cisalpine Gaul, but he was caught between two Roman armies, commanded by Gaius Antonius and Quintus Caecilius Metellus Celer. A bitter and violent battle ensued with heavy losses on both sides. Sallustius tells us that Catiline and his men fought with such ferocity and daring that practically every man was found dead upon the battle station that he had occupied before the battle began. Catiline, defiant as ever, was found at the head of his troops. Thus ended the conspiracy of Catiline in 62 B.C.

Also in 62 B.C., the Roman Senate trembled when it heard that Pompey with his well-seasoned, well-equipped army had landed at Brundisium, on the heel of the boot of Italy, and was on his way to Rome with an army of men who were devoted personally to Pompey and who were capable, at his word, of making him dictator. Pompey was at the apex of his power. Pompey relieved the fears of the Senate by voluntarily disbanding his army before he entered the city. The Senate no longer feared Pompey, now that he had disbanded his troops. The ungrateful Senate rejected his requests for land for his veterans, and for ratification of the agreements that he had made in Asia Minor while he was subjecting kingdoms and peoples to the control of Rome. As a result, Pompey, together with Crassus and other capitalists, were thrown into a flirtation with the Populares, and so, in the year 60 B.C., Pompey and Crassus, the richest man in Rome, and Julius Caesar, soon to rise to preeminence, reached an informal arrangement of power-sharing, known as the First Triumvirate.

Mr. President, the Roman Republic had been in existence, now, for a period of 693 years—lacking seven years of being seven centuries. It had only a few more years to run until its final collapse. The death rattle in its throat was not yet audible, but its vital signs had shown serious deterioration since the time of Tiberius Gracchus. Dominant individuals, helped by their supporters, struggled for power, prestige, and military glory. Incessant civil wars and wars in the provinces had extracted a terrible toll from the population of all Italy, and the price in blood and treasure was to flow through many generations.

The vanishing peasantry from the land, the declining family and religious values, the fading away of the old Roman virtues, a growing slave economy, power politics, graft and greed and venality and corruption in government, high unemployment and growing indolence—both of which had contributed to the swelling city mob—all of these were the signs as well as the elements of a creeping but certain decay of the republic.

[ 127 ]

Through it all, Mr. President, a weakened Senate—once the resplendent and supreme pillar of power undergirding the rugged, yet graceful architecture of the Roman republic—had lost its way, its nerve, its vision, and its independence. The Roman Senate—for so many centuries the pride of the republic—had failed at the critical junctures to demonstrate the firmness, the considered judgment, and the integrity that might not only have arrested, but might also have reversed, the decline of the republic. As of the year 60 B.C., the year of the First Triumvirate, the Senate possibly could even yet arrest and reverse the decline. But would it?

Mr. President, I yield the floor.

*Do not think it was by arms that our ancestors raised the State from so small beginnings to such grandeur. . . .*

*But there were other things from which they derived their greatness. . . . They were industrious at home, just rulers abroad, and to the Senate chamber they brought untrammeled minds, not enslaved by passion.*

Cato
(Speech in the Roman Senate demanding the death penalty for the accomplices of Catiline)

❧❧

*More states have perished by the violation of their moral customs than by the violation of their laws.*

Montesquieu

❧❧

*The accumulation of all powers, legislative, executive, and judiciary, in the same hands, whether of one, a few, or many, and whether hereditary, self-appointed, or elective, may justly be pronounced the very definition of tyranny.*

James Madison, *The Federalist No. 47*

[129]

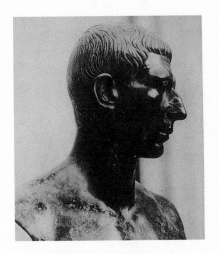

Cato the Younger

Gaius Julius Caesar

Marcus Tullius Cicero

Gnaeus Pompeius (Pompey)

# CHAPTER 11

# The Rise of Julius Caesar, 60–44 B.C.

*July 29, 1993*

Mr. BYRD. Mr. President, this is the eleventh in my series of speeches on the Roman political system of divided powers and checks and balances.

When Sulla had made himself master of Rome, he asked young Julius Caesar to repudiate his wife Cornelia, the daughter of Cinna. When Caesar refused to do so, Sulla considered having his name added to the proscription lists, but he was induced by someone to spare his life—the dictator reluctantly consenting, with the rejoinder that "their sagacity was small if they did not, in that boy, see many Marius's." Caesar considered it prudent to withdraw from Rome to Rhodes, and he did not return to Rome until after Sulla's death.

Caesar was chosen quaestor in 68 B.C., and assigned to serve in Spain. In 65 B.C., he was elected aedile. In 63 B.C., he was elected pontifex maximus, and in 62 B.C., praetor. In 61 B.C., he became propraetor for Spain, where he led many brilliant military campaigns against the tribes until he had made the whole country tributary to Rome and sent much money to the public treasury at Rome.

In 60 B.C., Caesar requested a triumph and also asked permission to stand as a candidate for the consulship while waiting outside the city to make a triumphal entry. Cato the Younger opposed this request and "used up the last day for the presentation of candidates in speech making," thus defeating Caesar's proposition. Here we see the example of an effective filibuster in the Roman Senate 2,053 years ago.

Caesar was, therefore, required to abandon his triumph, on the one hand, or, on the other, to enter the city and offer himself as a candidate for the consulship. He chose to abandon his triumph, entered the city, offered himself as a candidate, and was elected consul in 59 B.C.

Meanwhile, in 62 B.C., a victorious Pompey had returned from the East after a succession of military and diplomatic achievements and, contrary to the expectations of some, who feared that he would prove to be another Sulla, Pompey disbanded his army and entered Rome with no other retinue than his own personal staff. Thinking, perhaps naively, that the oligarchy would give him his due, Pompey pressed the Senate to ratify his arrangements that had been made in the East while he was winning victories for Rome, and also to provide land grants for about forty thousand veterans discharged from his legions. Without an army at his back, an ungrateful Senate no longer feared him and rejected both requests. To make bad matters worse, the Senate had also offended Crassus and the Equestrians by rejecting a request by the *publicani* to modify the terms of the contract for the collection of taxes in the province of Asia.

THE FIRST TRIUMVIRATE

These events rudely dashed Cicero's hopes for a concord of the orders. Taking full advantage of the situation, Julius Caesar, in 60 B.C., formed an unofficial coalition for power sharing with Pompey and Crassus, known as the First Triumvirate. It was an important turning point on the road to one-man rule in Rome, and was caused by an intransigent and unrealistic senatorial policy which threw these three men together.

Caesar, having been elected consul in 59 B.C., once in office, began to fulfill his commitments to his partners in the triumvirate. He brought in a law to provide lands for Pompey's veterans. Then he brought in another law ratifying the arrangements that Pompey had made in Asia Minor while fighting Rome's wars there. Caesar had now forced legislation through— over the opposition of the Senate—to carry out Pompey's wishes.

Although much of Caesar's legislation was determined by the interests of the triumvirate, he was also the author of some constructive legislation. One law, for example, provided protection for people in the Roman provinces against extortion by Roman officials. Among the innovations of Caesar, I shall mention one that may be of more than passing interest to my colleagues. This was a law that provided for the publication of senatorial resolutions in a kind of *Congressional Record* to prevent the garbling of official documents by unscrupulous magistrates. This record of senatorial proceedings was also meant to bring the Roman Senate under public scrutiny. These *acta diurna*, or "daily doings," were posted on the walls of the forums, and from these walls, the reports were copied and sent by messengers throughout all parts of Italy and the outlying provinces. This, again, might be of interest to my friends in the Senate, especially in the light of recent proposals to limit distribution of the *Congressional Record*, and to drastically reduce franked mail to our constituents. We seem to be going in the opposite direction from that in which Caesar was leading the Roman Senate in his time.

During Caesar's consulship, he laid the foundations for his future career by having a henchman named Publius Vatinius propose a law that was passed by the Tribal Assembly conferring upon Caesar the combined provinces of Cisalpine Gaul and Illyricum for a term of five years, ending on March 1, 54 B.C., with a garrison of three legions. In that same year of 59 B.C., during Caesar's consulship, the governor of Transalpine Gaul—Gaul, across the Alps—died. The Roman Senate, under pressure from Pompey, added that province to Caesar's command and gave him one more legion.

Caesar had greatly strengthened his position. He not only held a proconsular command in an area that offered the prospects for his winning military laurels, but the length of that term, five years, also assured him of immunity, for that period of time, from any attempt to hold him responsible for unconstitutional acts perpetrated during 59 B.C., the year of his consulship.

Before he left for Gaul in 58 B.C., Caesar selected a young aristocrat, Publius Clodius Pulcher, to act as his agent during his absence. Whatever Caesar's original intention had been,

[133]

his action resulted, figuratively speaking, in his tossing a fire-brand into the volatile city affairs. Rarely, if ever, had such a violent demagog been seen in Rome. Clodius demolished venerable constitutional safeguards, attacked the Senate, and converted low-priced grain for the Romans into a free dole, at great cost to the public treasury. He collected gangs of thugs, disrupted the civic order, and sent Cicero into exile. Caesar was prevailed upon by Pompey, however, to pardon Cicero, but Clodius delayed Cicero's return to Rome several months by bloody riots which continued even after Cicero's arrival back in Rome.

At a meeting which took place at Lucca, in northern Italy, in 56 B.C., Caesar renewed his pact with Crassus and Pompey. They agreed that Pompey should be made governor of Spain; that Crassus should be made governor of Syria; while Caesar, when his five-year term as governor of Gaul expired, should have his term extended for an additional five years to March 1, 49 B.C. Hurrying back to Gaul, Caesar crossed the Rhine in 55 B.C., for a brief show of force. In that same year, Caesar invaded Britain. He returned to Britain in 54 B.C., the following year, and vanquished the Britons in battle.

Rome had known Julius Caesar as a spendthrift, a rake, and a politician, but Rome was now amazed to find that Caesar was a very able and tireless administrator and a resourceful general. Caesar also showed himself at this time to be a historian. In the midst of his vigorous campaigns in Gaul, he recorded his conquest of Gaul in commentaries, the conciseness and simplicity of which constitute one of the great classics in military literature.

By his own accounts, Caesar could be merciful and he could be brutal. For example, after he had defeated the Atuatuci, he wrote that he "had the entire population sold at auction, in one lot, and the purchaser's returns showed a total of 53,000 souls." After the siege of Bourges, Caesar wrote that his troops "spared neither the aged nor women nor children. Indeed, from a total of some 40,000, a bare 800, who had fled at the first alarm, got through."

When Caesar began his eight-year-long Gallic wars, Rome's only communication with its holdings in Spain was along a narrow strip of the French Mediterranean coast which it controlled. Using superior Roman discipline and engineering skills, Caesar attacked and defeated each independent tribe separately, and by the time several tribes allied themselves to attack Roman forces, it was too late. Caesar's victories greatly extended Rome's enlightened influences, and paved the way, ultimately, for Caesar's seizure of power in Rome. All of Gaul, as far north as the Rhine River, had now been subjected to Rome, and for the next three hundred years, Gaul remained a Roman province.

Let us pause for a moment to reflect back to the time eleven weeks ago, when I spoke of Rome as being a tiny, fledgling rural community on the Tiber River in 753 B.C. Now we have seen Rome extend its dominions to include all of Italy and Spain, Gaul, the Balearic Islands, Carthage, Sicily, Sardinia, Illyricum, Macedonia, Greece, Corsica, Phrygia, Cilicia, Asia Minor, Bithynia, Pergamum, Pontus, Syria, Judea, and Numidia. A city-state was simply not equipped to administer such a sprawling empire, and the strains on Rome's resources, as we can imagine, were great, especially on her manpower.

In 54 B.C., Pompey's wife, Julia, who was Caesar's daughter, died and thus was severed an important bond between Caesar and Pompey. By then, Crassus was on his way to attack the Parthians. He crossed the Euphrates River and met the Parthians at Carrhae. A superior Parthian cavalry defeated Crassus. His son fell in the battle. Crassus was withdrawing his forces, when the Parthian leader invited him to a conference. Crassus went and was treacherously slain. His head was sent to the Parthian court, and only a few thousand men in his now leaderless army lived to make it back to Syria. A balancing force, as a result of the debacle of Crassus and his army, had been removed, for a victorious Crassus might have opposed the dictatorship of either Pompey or Caesar.

### CORRUPTION AND MOB RULE

Whereas we had a triumvirate, now we have two rivals remaining. While these two potential dictators were maneuvering for position, all of Rome was filled with the odor of a dying republic. The verdicts of juries, the offices of magistrates, and the votes of the assembly were sold to the highest bidders, and where money failed, murder was available.

Modern-era historian William Durant writes that crime flourished in the city, brigandage in the country, and no police force existed to control it. The lowest elements in Italy were attracted to Rome by the smell of money or the gift of corn, and any man who would vote as he was paid was admitted to the rolls, whether he was a citizen or not.

Gang warfare raged throughout Rome. We hear much today about gang warfare here in our own capital city and in other cities all over America. Clodius, we will remember, who was Caesar's agent, was murdered by a rival gang led by Titus Annius Papianus Milo, who had been engaged by Caesar's rival, Pompey.

A century of civil wars and revolution—beginning in 133 B.C., during the tribunate of Tiberius Gracchus—had broken down a selfish, arrogant oligarchy but had put no other government in its place.

We have seen the weakening of the Roman Senate. Unemployment, bribery, bread, and circuses corrupted the magistrates, the Assembly, and the Senate. Rome was at the mercy of an ill-informed and passion-ridden mob, incapable of ruling itself, much less an empire.

In March 49 B.C., Caesar's term as governor of Gaul would end, and he would be unable to run for consul until the fall of that year. In the interval, he would lose his immunity as an office holder and would not be able to enter Rome without subjecting himself to charges and trial by his political enemies. Cato, as a matter of fact, had already frankly expressed the hope that Caesar would be accused, tried, and banished from Italy.

Through his friends in the Senate, Caesar proposed that he be given permission to stand as a candidate for consul in absentia. The Senate refused to consider the motion and demanded that Caesar dismiss his troops. Caesar made a counterproposal, strange to say; he had no right to propose conditions on which he would lay down his command. But he made a counterproposal that both he and Pompey should lay down their commissions. The Senate supported the proposal, but Pompey balked at it. In the last days of the year 50 B.C., the Senate declared Julius Caesar a public enemy unless he should abandon his command by July 1 of the next year.

[136]

## CAESAR CROSSES THE RUBICON

Things went from bad to worse. After a long debate, the Roman Senate, persuaded by Cato and others, appointed Pompey dictator and voted him the money with which to collect a large army throughout Italy. It was expected that Caesar would require a few weeks to assemble his legions before becoming a major threat to Rome, but Caesar decided to seize the initiative and move quickly. On January 10 or 11—depending upon whether it was before midnight or after midnight—in the year 49 B.C., Caesar crossed the Rubicon, a small stream near Ariminum separating the rest of Italy from the southern boundary of Cisalpine Gaul.

Plutarch says that, before crossing the stream, Caesar stood silently for a while on its banks, reflecting on the dangers that would accompany the attempt which he was about to make, and "many times changed his opinion." Then, at last, by some sudden impulse, Plutarch says, Caesar cried out, "The die is cast," and immediately passed over the stream and reached Ariminum before daybreak and took it. The rest of his legions were expected to join him later.

All of Italy then became a state of turmoil. Bad news travels fast, and a wave of hysteria swept over Rome. Every new report was a report about the taking of this city or that city, and Pompey had no way to gain correct intelligence as to what was in fact going on. Those who lived outside the city fled from all quarters into the city, and those who were inside the city abandoned it in as much haste. Plutarch says that Pompey took the two consuls and fled, and that "most of the Senators snatched up those things in their houses that were next at hand and joined him in the flight."

"What a miserable spectacle was the city then!" says Plutarch, "in so dreadful a tempest, like a ship abandoned by its pilots, tossed about at all adventures, and at the mercy of the winds and seas." Caesar pursued Pompey, who, as leader of the republican forces, had sent part of his army and the two consuls across the Adriatic to Dyrrachium. Pompey sailed from Brundisium upon the approach of Caesar and joined the rest of his army in Macedonia. Caesar would have followed him, but, because he lacked the ships, he was unable to do so.

[137]

Plutarch recounts that Caesar returned to Rome after having reduced all of Italy "without spilling a drop of blood." Caesar then sought the keys to the public treasury, and when Metellus, a tribune, cited certain laws that were against it, Caesar said, "Arms and laws do not flourish together," and threatened to slay Metellus if he did not stand aside. Then, Caesar sent for the workmen to open the doors and readily supplied himself with the resources necessary to fight the war. He then proceeded to defeat Pompey's forces in Spain, so that he would not have an army at his back when he later would move against Pompey in Asia.

Upon Caesar's return from Spain in 49 B.C., the rump Senate made him dictator. After taking certain actions, such as recalling all those who were in exile, and relieving debtors by canceling part of the interest on their debts, Caesar laid down his dictatorship at the end of eleven days. He then caused himself to be declared consul, along with Publius Servilius Isauricus, and promptly left Rome to prosecute the war.

Even though it was in the midst of winter and Pompey controlled the Adriatic, Caesar was able, at great risks, to move his army across the Adriatic, and to engage Pompey's forces in battle. At Dyrrachium, Caesar was defeated by Pompey. But Pompey failed to give the finishing stroke. He sent his army right up to the camp of Caesar after Caesar's defeat, but Plutarch says that, for some unknown reason, "either through too much caution or the caprice of fortune," instead of delivering the finishing stroke, Pompey sounded a retreat. That night, Caesar said to his men, "This day, victory would have declared for the enemy if they had had a general who knew how to conquer."

CAESAR VICTORIOUS

Caesar retreated with his defeated army into Thessaly, followed by Pompey. Pompey's fleet of five hundred large ships and many more smaller ones controlled the lines of supply from the sea. But he favored a protraction of the war by avoiding an all-out battle with Caesar's troops who, although they were greatly outnumbered, were seasoned veterans and supremely dedicated to Caesar.

[138]

Pompey now made a decision that would cost him his life. Although he favored the old Fabian strategy of delay, which had been used against Hannibal by Fabius Maximus Cunctator, his officer corps, made up of senators and other aristocrats, were overly confident. They had just defeated Caesar's forces and believed the war should be brought to an end quickly. But Pompey thought it best to delay. He knew he controlled the lines of supply; he knew that after a little while, Caesar's forces would run out of supplies and would become famished, threatened with hunger. But Plutarch says that not a man agreed with Pompey except Cato, and they taunted Pompey with aspersions of cowardice. Piqued by these reproaches, Pompey, against his own better judgment, gave the order to do battle.

As the battle lines were forming on the plains of Pharsalia, Caesar saw a trusty centurion, and calling him by name, said, "What cheer, Caius Crastinus? How, think you, do we stand?" "Caesar," replied the veteran in a bold accent, and stretching out his hand, "this day you will gain a glorious victory. As for me, whether alive or dead, I shall deserve the praises of Caesar." So saying, the centurion departed and led his company with great daring, pressing the enemy with great fierceness, until one of Pompey's men saw him approaching and waited to receive him, thrusting his sword into his mouth with such force that it went through the nape of his neck. Crastinus was killed, but Caesar's troops were victorious.

The battle of Pharsalus was fought on August 9, 48 B.C. Pompey and his forces were routed, after which Caesar took over Pompey's camp and killed those left in charge of it, most of whom were slaves. Pompey then fled to Larissa, where he took a ship to Egypt, having been joined by his wife Cornelia and his son.

Pompey was treacherously stabbed to death by the Egyptians when he set foot on the Egyptian shore. His assassination was in full view of his wife, who had remained on the vessel that had transported them to Egypt. She was able to escape the pursuing Egyptians only with the help of a brisk gale. Thus, Mr. President, was the sad end of Pompey the Great.

Caesar pursued Pompey to Egypt but, of course, arrived too late. Caesar became involved in a war with Ptolemy XIII, the result of which was the defeat of Ptolemy and his death by drowning, and the establishment of Cleopatra VII, Ptolemy's sister, and now Caesar's mistress, on the throne as queen. Plutarch tells us that Cleopatra later bore Caesar a son named Caesarion.

Plutarch also tells us how Cleopatra was removed from the city by Photinus, the Egyptian vizier, and how, in the dusk of evening, she returned to the city in a small boat and rolled herself up in a carpet and was carried like a bale of goods by Apollodorus, a Sicilian, through the gates of the palace to Caesar.

After Caesar defeated the Egyptians, he proceeded into Asia Minor, where he defeated Pharnaces II, the son of Mithridates VI Eupator, at the battle of Zela in 47 B.C. This was the battle that occasioned the famous boast by Caesar: "Veni, Vidi, Vici"—"I came, I saw, I conquered."

At Thapsus, on April 6, 46 B.C., Caesar met and defeated the combined forces of Metellus Scipio, Cato, Titus Labienus, and Juba I, the king of the Numidians. Juba committed suicide after the battle. Scipio fled and later died in an engagement at sea. But Cato managed to escape with a portion of his army to Utica, which lay just a bit northwest of Carthage. Later, Cato's officers wanted to defend Utica against Caesar, but Cato persuaded them that it was impossible. He urged all Romans to flee, and he offered to provide funds for their flight. But he urged his own son to submit to Caesar. Cato, for himself, however, rejected both courses.

Upon Caesar's approach, Cato spent the evening in philosophical discussion, then retired to his room and read Plato's *Phaedo*, a dialogue on the immortality of the soul. His friends, suspicious that Cato would kill himself, removed his sword from his bedside. Cato demanded that it be returned, and it was sent back into his room by a little boy. Cato examined the sword, found the point and the edge good, and then said, "Now I am master of myself."

Then, Cato picked up the book again and read it some more, after which, Plutarch says, he slept until about midnight. When he awakened, he called two of his freedmen, Cleanthes, a physician, and Butas. He asked Butas to go to the port and determine whether or not all of the Romans had gotten

[140]

off to sea, and to bring him word. When Butas returned and informed him that everyone had gotten off, with the exception of one individual who was briefly detained by personal business, Cato fell again into a light slumber.

As the slender golden fingers of dawn began to pierce the black veil of the night, and the birds began to sing, Cato drew the sword and plunged it into his own abdomen. His friends rushed into the room, and the physician began to sew up the wound. But as Cato came a little to himself, he thrust the physician away, tore open the wound and expired immediately. Cato died when he was 48 years old—a man whose constitutionalism was a mixture of stoicism and old Roman virtues, a constitutionalism that was genuine.

### A Frightened Senate Thrusts Power on Caesar

Caesar returned to Rome in the fall of 46 B.C., where a frightened Senate voted him the dictatorship for ten years. Two years later, the Senate made him dictator for life. Caesar threw many feasts and entertained many people. Upon one occasion, he set 22,000 tables. But he had another war to fight, so he went off, in 45 B.C., to Munda in Spain, and defeated the two sons of Pompey. The older son was killed; the younger son escaped. After the battle, Caesar said he had often fought for victory, but this was the first time he had fought for his life.

Caesar returned to Rome. As dictator, he enlarged the Senate from six hundred members to nine hundred. He reformed the local government, and introduced the Julian calendar in 46 B.C., by making that year a year of fifteen months. The supply of free corn was radically reduced, and Caesar attempted to settle more freedmen on small farms throughout Italy.

There was no military, legislative, administrative, or financial authority in Rome that Caesar did not completely control. He had the power to declare war or peace without consulting the once great Roman Senate. Caesar had sole power over the purse, which, through the centuries, as we recall, the Roman Senate had completely controlled. Caesar was above the law. No magistrate could be sworn into office, except he first swore that he would uphold the acts of Caesar.

Caesar was master of the Senate, master of Rome, master of all Italy, and master of the Roman world. But Caesar's mastery would abruptly end on the Ides of March, 44 B.C., when the blood from "three and twenty wounds" would extinguish his life, and stain the pedestal of the statue of Pompey in the Roman Senate house—proof once again that, by diverse means, all men come to the same end.

I yield the floor.

*After a century of civil wars and revolution, Rome was exhausted. . . .[F]arms had been neglected, much of the countryside had been left desolate, small towns had been deserted, the cities had been besieged and sacked, robbers and gangs had left the streets unsafe, morals had eroded, adulteries and divorces had multiplied, and a shallow sophistication prided itself upon its arrogant cynicism—much of what we see in our own country today. [page 155]*

*Assassination of Caesar*

# CHAPTER 12

# The Senate: Little More Than a Name, 46–23 B.C.

*September 7, 1993*

Mr. BYRD. Mr. President, this is the twelfth in my series of speeches on the line-item veto, with particular emphasis on the Roman constitution and its influence upon the United States Constitution. In my last speech on this subject, which was delivered just before the August recess, I spoke of the formulation of the First Triumvirate in 60 B.C.—an unofficial, power-sharing arrangement among Julius Caesar, Marcus Licinius Crassus, and Gneus Pompeius Magnus, or Pompey the Great.

I also spoke of the death of Crassus, one of the triumvirs, in 53 B.C.; of the crossing of the Rubicon by Caesar in 49, and his defeat of the other triumvir, Pompey, at the battle of Pharsalus in 48 B.C. I spoke of the battle of Thapsus, the death of Cato, and the rise to the pinnacle of power by Caesar in 46 B.C., when he was made dictator for ten years.

### DEGRADATION OF THE SENATE

Mr. President, from July 28, 46 B.C., to March 15, 44 B.C., Julius Caesar ruled the Roman world. His autocratic position derived from the support of the military elements, including the veterans of his many successful military campaigns, and from the excessive powers he acquired through the various offices fulsomely conferred upon him by a servile Senate, foremost among which was the dictatorship, which he had held for a brief time in 49 B.C., and again in 47. In 46 B.C., he was made dictator for ten years, and in 44 B.C., for life.

[ 145 ]

Simultaneously, Caesar was consul. He also enjoyed the personal inviolability of the tribunes, and, in 46 B.C., he was given the powers of censorship for life—note that I said he was "given" the powers of censorship—and the sole power over the purse—get that! One man—Caesar—had the sole power over the public purse!

Cicero was the first who proposed that the Senate should give special powers and honors to Caesar, and those who followed contended with each other as to which could pay the most extraordinary compliments to Caesar.

According to the historian Cassius Dio Cocceianus, senators voted Caesar the title Father of his Country, stamped this title on the coinage, renamed the month Quintilis, in which he was born, Julian, or July, and voted to celebrate his birthday by public sacrifice. Additionally, they ordered that he should have a statue in the cities and in all the temples of Rome, that another Senate house be named The Julian, and that all his future acts should be regarded as valid in advance. They voted that he should always ride, even in the city itself, wearing the triumphal dress, and sitting in his chair of state everywhere except at the games. When Caesar kept refusing the title of "king," and rebuking, in a way, those who thus accosted him, yet did nothing by which it could be thought that he was really displeased at it all, they secretly adorned his statue, which stood on the rostra, with a diadem.

CONSPIRACY

Dio writes: "A baleful frenzy fell upon certain men through jealousy of his advancement, and hatred of his preferment to themselves caused his death unlawfully, while it added a new name to the annals of infamy." Many of the senators in the old ruling oligarchy were bitter at his manifestations of disdain toward the Senate. He once received them sitting, which roused great indignation among them all.

Among these disgruntled elements, a conspiracy was formed against the life of the dictator. The originator of the plot was Gaius Cassius Longinus, an ex-Pompeiian who had been named praetor by Caesar, and who was joined by Marcus Junius Brutus, another ex-Pompeiian, both of whom had fought against

[146]

Caesar at the battle of Pharsalus, and both of whom had been pardoned by him.

Marcus Junius Brutus was reputed to be a descendant of Lucius Junius Brutus, who had led in the expulsion of Tarquin the Proud in 510 B.C., and who had been chosen as the first consul of the newly founded republic in 509 B.C. Marcus Brutus was also the nephew and son-in-law of Cato the Younger, and was highly regarded by Caesar. It was generally believed that Caesar was the father of Brutus, inasmuch as Caesar had had amorous relations with Servilia, the mother of Brutus, which, according to Plutarch, were in "full bloom" at about the time Brutus was born.

When Gaius Cassius solicited his friends to join in the conspiracy, they consented on the condition that Brutus would take the lead. They wanted a man of high reputation to preside over the assassination so that the world would see the deed as having had an honorable purpose.

Cassius was married to Junia, the sister of Brutus, and was a man of violent passions. He possessed a deep aversion to tyrants. As it had been reported that the friends of Caesar designed to move that he be declared king on the calends of March, the first day of the month, Cassius asked Brutus what his intentions would be in that event. Brutus, who would one day remind Cicero that "our ancestors scorned to bear even a gentle master," answered Cassius, according to Plutarch, saying, "It would be my duty, not only to speak against it, but to sacrifice my life for the liberties of Rome." From that point on, the two proceeded to talk with their trusted friends. Among those who concurred in the plot was another Brutus, Decimus Junius Brutus, surnamed Albinus. It was decided that the assassination would take place at a meeting of the Senate on the ides of March, the 15th day of the month.

Caesar had some suspicions concerning Cassius, says Plutarch, and even said one day to some friends that he did not fear "fat and sleek" men but, rather, feared "pale and lean" ones. Shakespeare has him saying to Antonius:

Let me have men about me that are fat;
Sleek-headed men and such as sleep o'nights;
Yond' Cassius has a lean and hungry look;
He thinks too much. Such men are dangerous.

[ 147 ]

A certain soothsayer had forewarned Caesar that a great danger threatened him on the ides of March, and Caesar's friends pressed him to have a bodyguard, but Caesar did not allow it, saying that it was "better to die once than to live always in fear of death." Shakespeare deftly shapes the words of Caesar as he brushes aside Calpurnia's fears for his safety: "Cowards die many times before their deaths. The valiant never taste of death but once."

On the evening before the ides of March, Caesar supped at the house of Marcus Aemilius Lepidus, his master of the horse, and, as he sat at the table, there arose a question, "What kind of death is best?" Caesar, answering before all others, cried out, "A sudden one."

That night, Calpurnia dreamed that she was weeping over him as she held him, murdered, in her arms. The next morning, she conjured Caesar not to go out that day, but Decimus Brutus, in whom Caesar placed great confidence, had come to escort him to the Senate and prevailed upon him to go.

On the way to the Senate, Artemidorus the Cnidian, who had gotten wind of the conspiracy, approached Caesar with a paper, and pressing up as close as possible to him, said, "Read this to yourself, and quickly, for it contains matters of great consequence and concern to you." Caesar took the paper, but he was denied the opportunity of reading it by one thing or another from those around him.

As Caesar entered the Senate house, all of the senators rose to do him honor. As he took his seat, all of the conspirators came up to his chair and pretended to intercede, along with Tullus Cimber for the recall of his brother from exile. As they continued their importunities, Caesar answered them with a blunt negative and then grew angry. Cimber then, with both hands, pulled Caesar's purple robe off his neck, which was the signal for the attack.

Publius Servilius Casca gave him the first blow—a stroke upon the neck with his dagger. All of the conspirators now drew their daggers, so that, whatever way Caesar turned, he saw nothing but steel gleaming in his face and met nothing but wounds from Cassius, Bucolianus, Brutus, and others. Caesar struggled against the assassins, but, it is related by the historian Suetonius, that Caesar gave up the struggle against

[148]

his murderers when, seeing Brutus among them, he exclaimed in Greek, *"kai su, teknon?"*—"even you, my child?" The Latin version *"et tu, Brute?"*—"even you, Brutus?"—was made famous by Shakespeare.

Caesar then wrapped his robe around his face, composed himself for death, and yielded to his fate. He expired upon the pedestal of Pompey's statue and dyed it with his blood, so that Pompey seemed to preside over the work of vengeance, to tread his enemy under his feet, and to enjoy his agonies. Caesar died of "no less than three and twenty wounds." In all, some sixty senators had shared in the conspiracy.

Mr. President, the assassination of Julius Caesar was one of the most momentous happenings in the history of the world, and it ended the life of one of the most remarkable men who has ever lived.

Plutarch's words here are particularly penetrating:

> Julius Caesar died at the age of 56. His object was sovereign power and authority, which he pursued through innumerable dangers, and by prodigious efforts, he gained it at last. But he reaped no other fruit from it than an empty and invidious title.
>
> It is true that the Divine Power, which conducted him through life, attended him after his death as his avenger; pursued and hunted out the assassins over sea and land; and rested not till there was not a man left, either of those who had dipped their hands in his blood, or of those who gave their sanction to the deed.

Mr. President, we are familiar—through Shakespeare and others—with Mark Antony's funeral oration and also with the reading of Caesar's will, which named as his adopted son and successor his grandnephew, Gaius Octavius Caepias, who then took the name Gaius Julius Caesar Octavianus, or Octavian as he is generally known.

### The Second Triumvirate

In 43 B.C.—the year following Ceasar's death—Lepidus, who was now governor of Nearer Spain and of Gallia Narbonensis, or Narbonese Gaul, arranged a conference with Antony and Octavian which took place on a small islet in a river—Appian calls it the Lavinius River; another historian calls it the Renus

River; but those names have long since changed—that flowed near Mutina, now modern Modena, where they agreed on a joint policy. They declared themselves an executive committee, the Second Triumvirate, with absolute powers for five years, for the reconstruction of the Roman state, and divided the provinces among themselves.

The triumvirs—in order to pay their soldiers, build up their coffers, avenge Caesar, and destroy their opponents—sent shock waves throughout Roman society by a proscription that was as cold-blooded and loathsome as that of Sulla, about which I spoke on a previous occasion.

Among their victims were three hundred Senators and two thousand knights. The excuse alleged was the avenging of the murder of Caesar. But the real reasons were the destruction of their political enemies, and the confiscation of wealth and property in order to raise money for their forthcoming campaign against Brutus and Cassius.

Throughout town and country, there was terrible panic. The heads of all the victims were displayed on the rostrum in the Forum, where it was necessary to bring them to the triumvirs in order to collect the rewards. In the effort to escape, some of the proscribed descended into wells, others into filthy sewers; some sought refuge in chimneys; some died defending themselves against their murderers; and some hanged or starved or drowned themselves. Of those who made their escape, some perished in shipwrecks, ill-luck pursuing them to the last.

Their most famous victim was Cicero. Appian says that Cicero was killed near Capua, but Valerius Maximus says that the scene of that tragedy was Cajeta. Cicero was being carried in a litter by his servants when the assassins came up. Plutarch tells us that Cicero saw Herennius, a centurian, approaching, and ordered his servants to let him down. And placing his hand to his chin, as was his custom to do, he gazed steadfastly upon his murderers. Herennius dispatched Cicero as he stretched his neck out of the litter to catch the blow; thus, Cicero fell in his sixty-fourth year of age.

Herennius then cut off Cicero's head, and, in accordance with the command that had previously been given by Antony, also cut off the hand that had written the *Philippics*, Cicero's orations against Antony.

[150]

When these parts of Cicero's body were brought to Rome, Antony was conducting an assembly for the election of magistrates. Overjoyed by the sight of the head and hand of his hated enemy, Antony rewarded Herennius with a bonus amounting to ten times the normal price of 25,000 attic drachmas paid per head.

Cassius Dio Cocceianus, a historian, tells us that Fulvia, wife of Antony, took Cicero's head into her hands, and, after spitefully abusing it and spitting upon it, placed it upon her knees, opened the mouth, and, pulling out the tongue, pierced it with the pins she had used in her hair, all the time uttering many brutal jests.

Antony then ordered that the head and the hand be fastened up over the rostrum in the Forum, where Cicero had delivered his *Philippics*—a sad spectacle to the Roman people, who thought that they did not so much see the face of Cicero as a picture of Antony's soul.

### PHILIPPI: A DECISIVE VICTORY

After crushing all resistance in Italy, the triumvirates determined to make war on Brutus and Cassius who, with nineteen legions, had taken up a strong position at Philippi, in northeast Macedonia, and whose fleets dominated the seas. Leaving Lepidus to watch over Rome and Italy, and eluding the republican naval patrols, Antony and Octavian landed in Greece with twenty-eight legions and advanced to Philippi.

Plutarch relates that, when Brutus and Cassius were departing from Asia and on their way to Philippi, Brutus had seen an extraordinary apparition. He was sitting alone in his tent, reading and tending to business by a dim light and at a late hour. The whole army lay in sleep and in silence, while Brutus, wrapped in meditation, thought he perceived something enter his tent. Turning toward the door, he saw a horrible, monstrous specter standing silently by his side. "What art thou?" asked Brutus boldly. "Art thou god or man? And what is thy business with me?" The specter answered him, "I am thy evil genius, Brutus. Thou wilt see me at Philippi," to which Brutus calmly replied, "I will meet thee there."

In the first battle at Philippi, Brutus faced the forces of Octavian, while Cassius was opposite Antony's wing. Brutus

[ 151 ]

was victorious over Octavian, but the left wing, under Cassius, was overcome by Antony. In this circumstance, Brutus failed to relieve Cassius because Brutus knew not that Cassius needed relief. Brutus did not have our little cellular telephones in that day, else he would have known, and the outcome of the battle might have been different.

When Brutus had destroyed the camp of Octavian and could see no sign of Cassius, he sent a large detachment of cavalry to relieve Cassius, who had been forced to retire with a small number to a hill overlooking the plain. Cassius was nearsighted. He could not see clearly at a distance, but his companions saw a large detachment of horsemen approaching, which Cassius concluded to be the enemy in pursuit of him. He, therefore, sent his faithful friend Titinius to reconnoiter them. As the cavalry of Brutus saw Cassius's friend approach, some of them leaped from their horses and embraced him, while others came up around him, amidst clashing of arms and expressions of gladness. Cassius mistook what he saw to be the seizure of his loyal friend, Titinius, by the enemy, and he regretted having sent Titinius into the enemy's hands. He then withdrew to an empty tent, accompanied by his freedman, Pindarus, where Cassius killed himself with the same dagger that he had plunged into the veins of Caesar. Cassius died on his birthday.

At the second battle of Philippi, Brutus was defeated. After the battle, he retired to the top of a large rock where he presented his naked sword to his breast and, with the help of his trusted friend, Strato, fell upon his sword and died.

The republicans had lost the last great land battle. Philippi was a decisive victory. It laid the entire Roman world at the victor's feet. To Antony, the real victor, belonged the glory and the major portion of the spoils. As for Lepidus, Antony and Octavian shunted him off to Africa, where he slid into impotence and obscurity.

ANTONY AND CLEOPATRA

The pressures of time prevent me from dwelling on the momentous years that transpired between the battles of Philippi and the battle of Actium. Antony had spent several of those years in the east, where he had failed in a campaign against

[ 152 ]

the Parthians, finally limping back to Syria after having lost twenty thousand men. He would have lost more men had it not been for his superb generalship and the discipline of his legions. Meanwhile, he had been completely captivated by the personal charm of Cleopatra VII, whom Julius Caesar had established on the Egyptian throne as queen.

Antony had come to Tarsus—we remember Paul of Tarsus—in Cilicia, where Cleopatra, whom he had previously summoned to explain why she had aided and financed the conspirators, was soon to arrive. Cleopatra arrived in a splendid barge with silvery oars and purple sails. She was all decked out in gorgeous clothes, redolent with exquisite perfumes. Without questioning her past policies, Antony quickly succumbed to the spell of her irresistible charm.

The love life of Antony was only a pretext for the struggle between Antony and Octavian. It is true that Antony had treated his wife Octavia, the sister of Octavian, in a shabby manner. She had been a good and loyal wife, and Antony's rejection and divorce of her were abominable to many Romans; for Octavian, they constituted a personal insult and an act of war. The breach between the two rivals constantly widened, and the propaganda machine of Octavian worked overtime, day and night, against Antony and Cleopatra.

It was not easy for so crafty a politician as Octavian to go to war against a man as popular as Antony, with both consuls on his side and half of the Senate. To prove Antony a menace to Rome was a difficult thing to do. But Cleopatra was another matter. Cleopatra was more vulnerable, and against her, Octavian's propaganda machine would more effectively work. Was not that detestable oriental queen plotting to make herself empress over the Roman world? Had she not been heard to say that she would one day hand down justice from the Capitol? In all of Cleopatra's alleged machinations, Antony was made to appear as her doting dupe.

Capitalizing on the popular revulsion against Antony and Cleopatra, Octavian now moved to mobilize public opinion. He contrived to secure, from the municipalities in Italy and the provinces, an oath of personal allegiance, after which he declared Antony stripped of his Imperium and of his consulate.

Late in the fall of 32 B.C., Octavian declared war. Antony, meanwhile, had sailed for Greece where he took up a strong position at Actium. Militarily, Antony should have won the battle of Actium. He was the superior general, and his land forces were at least the equal of Octavian's. He also had a large naval fleet. But Antony's weaknesses outweighed his strengths. Not one of his admirals was the equal of Marcus Vipsanius Agrippa, Octavian's great naval commander. Moreover, Antony's ships were too heavy and too slow. But, worst of all was the low morale of his forces. His officers detested Cleopatra, and, in private, they cursed Antony for not sending her back to Egypt.

The battle of Actium was fought on September 2, 31 B.C., and is considered to be one of the most famous and decisive battles of the world. Yet, it evidently was a miserable affair and scarcely worthy of the name of battle. It was fought at sea, and only a small number of ships actually were engaged. The land armies never fought at all. The battle of Actium was decisive and famous only because it marked the end of the republic and foreordained the beginning of the empire.

At the height of the already hopeless battle, Antony caught sight of Cleopatra's ship withdrawing from the contest and heading out to sea. The reason for her precipitous departure is not known, but the distraught Antony instantly followed his queen—who was the first cause, and now the accomplisher, of his ruin. His men, left leaderless, soon succumbed to bewilderment and surrender.

The following year, 30 B.C., Antony committed suicide in Egypt. Shortly thereafter, Cleopatra took her own life. Cleopatra died at age 39. Antony was 47—some say older—when he died.

Shortly before Cleopatra expired, she had had brought to her, concealed in a basket of figs, some poisonous asps. Shakespeare has Cleopatra saying to her faithful lady attendant Iras: "Give me my robe; put on my crown; I have immortal longings in me," after which she presses one of the poisonous asps to her breast, it bites her, and she dies.

## THE RISE OF AUGUSTUS

Late in the summer of 29 B.C., Octavian returned to Rome in triumph. After a century of civil wars and revolution, Rome was exhausted. Historian Will Durant relates that farms had been neglected, much of the countryside had been left desolate, small towns had been deserted, the cities had been besieged and sacked, robbers and gangs had left the streets unsafe, morals had eroded, adulteries and divorces had multiplied, and a shallow sophistication prided itself upon its arrogant cynicism—much of what we see in our own country today.

The Senate by now was little more than a name. In Durant's words, it "gratefully yielded its major powers to one who would plan, accept responsibility, and lead." And out of the collapse of the republic, it was necessary to form a new government that would forge a new order. Step by step, Octavian persuaded—or, perhaps to be more accurate, he graciously permitted the Senate and the Assembly to cede him powers which, in their totality, made him king in everything but name.

Octavian revised the membership of the Senate and expelled some two hundred of the more disreputable senators. (In 18 B.C., the process of deflation was continued when he reduced the number of senators to six hundred.) On the 13th of January, 27 B.C., Octavian appeared before the purged Senate, proclaimed the restoration of the republic, dramatically offered to give up all of his powers to the Senate and the people, and expressed the desire, at thirty-five years of age, to retire to private life. Overwhelmed by the noble gesture, the Senate countered his offer of abdication with its own abdication, restored to him nearly all of his powers, and implored him to continue his guidance of the Roman state.

Three days later, on the 16th of January, 27 B.C., the Roman Senate conferred upon Octavian the title of "Augustus," by which he was henceforth known. It was a term that conveyed no new powers, but was an epithet applicable to the gods and to all things holy, and was well adapted to his exalted position. This term of exalted connotation and religious association made Augustus larger than life and worthy of veneration as a sacred being.

A second title was conferred, that of "imperator," which, after 27 B.C., Augustus used as a permanent praenomen. The

[155]

praenomen "imperator," after that time, was the prerogative of every Roman commander in chief. From the term "imperator" derived the term "emperor," commonly used today to designate Augustus and his successors.

Augustus was the president of the Senate—the *Princeps Senatus*—first among senators. But he was also designated *princeps civium Romanorum*, first among Roman citizens. From the word "princeps" arose the term "principate"—to designate the office held by the princeps, a term which also applies to the system of government which Augustus established for the empire.

In 27 B.C., Augustus established a committee to assist him in preparing the agenda for the meetings of the Senate. The committee consisted of both consuls, a representative of each of the other magistracies, and fifteen senators chosen by lot and rotating every six months. Reinforced by members of the imperial family and the Equestrian order in 13 A.D., the committee began to assume many of the formal functions belonging to the Senate.

Also in 27 B.C., Augustus created the Praetorian Guard, a permanent corps of nine cohorts, or battalions, each one thousand strong, of picked soldiers to serve as the emperor's guards and to accompany the emperor and his family wherever they went, and also to perform the miscellaneous functions of imperial aides-de-camp. Three of the cohorts were billeted about the city. The remainder were quartered in nearby towns. For several years, Augustus kept them under his direct control. But in the year 2 B.C., the command was entrusted to two *praefecti praetorio*, or praetorian prefects.

Lucius Aelius Sejanus was made joint prefect with his father upon the accession of Tiberius in 14 A.D., and was made sole prefect in 16 or 17 A.D. By 23 A.D., Sejanus had succeeded in concentrating all of the guard in one barracks near the Porta Viminalis, from which event dates the political importance of the Praetorian Guard and its commanders.

Caligula increased the number of cohorts to twelve, and under Vitellius they grew to sixteen. Vespasian reverted to nine; Domitian raised the number to ten, where it remained significantly unchanged until the Praetorian Guard was disbanded by Constantine the Great in 312 A.D.

[ 156 ]

Now, I have mentioned the guard here because, in the future centuries of empire following Augustus, the guard would prove to be a fertile hotbed for sedition and conspiracy, and would, from time to time, make and break emperors. As a matter of fact, Sejanus, who had been the first sole prefect, was executed by Tiberius for leading a conspiracy.

In 23 B.C., Augustus reached a new settlement, or understanding, with the Senate. His powers were vastly increased at home and abroad. He was granted the tribunition power, and was also granted the Imperium over the city, over the whole empire, and over the army. Thus, all of the powers of the Roman state were now vested in one man, the emperor, whose word was law.

The Senate ceded—note the word "ceded," the Senate was not forced to do it—the Senate ceded to Augustus special authority to conclude treaties with foreign powers without submitting them to the Senate or to the people for ratification. All incoming magistrates swore an oath to observe all of the emperor's acts and ordinances, past and future. As the master of the legions he was also their paymaster. He controlled the purse strings of the Roman state, and his was the determining voice in all questions of taxation. Augustus also acquired the appellate jurisdiction, and the habit of "appealing unto Caesar" gradually established the Imperial Court of Appeal as a regular part of the Roman constitution. Thus, in 23 B.C., were forged the two constitutional bases of the principate: The tribunition power and the proconsular Imperium.

The constitution of the empire dates from the year 23 B.C. Thus, 23 B.C. marks the birth of the Roman empire, and Augustus apparently recognized its significance, for he dated all future public documents from that year, 23 B.C.

The emperor enjoyed absolute power and authority as a gift of the Senate and the people, technically speaking, but, in reality, the wide range and magnitude of his powers and functions were essentially monarchical. Rome, which had been founded by a legendary king, beginning in 753 B.C., and had been ruled by historical kings until 510 B.C., was now, 730 years later, in 23 B.C., governed by an emperor. The Roman Senate which, for almost five centuries, controlled the power of the purse and had been the supreme organ under the republic, had voluntarily given up these powers, had become dependent, had become fearful, had lost its nerve, and had ceded power, without being forced to do so, to an emperor. And for the next 499 years, ending in the year 476 A.D., Rome would be governed by emperors.

Rome had gone the full circle, from king, to republic, to emperor. But, "What's in a name?" That which we call a king, by any other name would be the same.

I thank the Chair and yield the floor.

*The victory over the senate was easy and inglorious. Every eye and every passion was directed to the supreme magistrate, who possessed the arms and treasure of the state; whilst the senate, neither elected by the people, nor guarded by military force, nor animated by public spirit, rested its declining authority on the frail and crumbling basis of ancient opinion.*

Edward Gibbon, *The Decline and Fall of the Roman Empire*

 જ્યજ્ય

*In order to judge of the form to be given to this institution [the Senate], it will be proper to take a view of the ends to be served by it. These were,—first, to protect the people against their rulers, secondly, to protect the people against the transient impressions into which they themselves might be led.*

James Madison, *Journal of the Federal Convention*

 જ્યજ્ય

*There are particular moments in public affairs, when the people, stimulated by some irregular passion . . . or misled by the artful misrepresentations of interested men, may call for measures which they themselves will afterwards be the most ready to lament and condemn. In these critical moments, how salutary will be the interference of some temperate and respectable body of citizens in order to . . . suspend the blow meditated by the people against themselves, until reason, justice, and truth can regain their authority over the public mind? What bitter anguish would not the people of Athens have often escaped if their government had contained so provident a safeguard against the tyranny of their own passions? Popular liberty might then have escaped the indelible reproach of decreeing to the same citizens, the hemlock on one day, and statues on the next.*

James Madison, *The Federalist No. 63*
(in reference to the Senate)

[159]

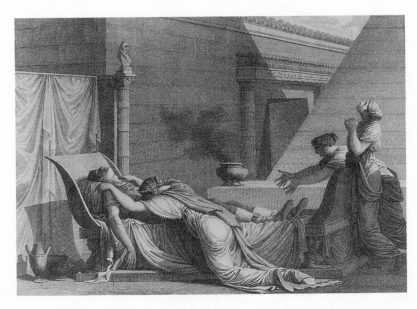

*Death of Antony*

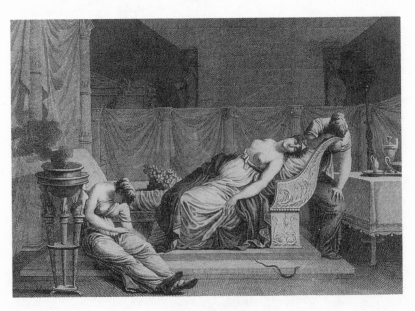

*Death of Cleopatra*

# CHAPTER 13

# A Turbulent Stream Flowing through Dark Centuries of Intrigue and Violence

*September 20, 1993*

Mr. BYRD. Madam President, this is the thirteenth in my series of speeches on the line-item veto, with particular emphasis on the Roman republic and the Roman Senate.

### The Senate's Surrender to Caesar

For centuries, the Roman Senate was a body of the wisest, the best educated, the most respected, most experienced, most vigilant, most patriotic men of substance in the Roman republic.

In the beginning, the Senate acted as an advisory council to the monarchs, but over time it attained the pinnacle of majesty until, indeed, the symbol of Roman state authority was scripted SPQR, *Senatus Populusque Romanus*. This was the stamp of approval, of power and authority under which the victorious Roman legions marched with their golden eagles as they conquered the Mediterranean world.

The Roman Senate had complete control over the purse. It determined foreign policy, executed foreign policy, made and ratified treaties. It approved or disapproved legislation. It approved the elections of magistrates, and it determined who would be entrusted with the powers of dictator in a time of crisis for the Roman state. The Roman Senate was the guardian of the Roman state. It was the conscience of the republic.

Rome had no written constitution as we know it. Precedents were set and understood and followed by tradition and custom.

[161]

Precedent had developed a little-used but dangerous office—the office of dictator. Roman custom had allowed for the designation of a dictator for a period of not to exceed six months, from whose order no appeal was allowed, whose word was law for the duration of his tenure, who held the powers of life and death over every Roman citizen, and who held the supreme command over the Roman military forces.

In 82 B.C., upon seizure of the reins of power in Rome, Sulla had himself appointed dictator for an indeterminate term. For our purposes, Sulla might be described as an early and comparable equivalent of Benito Mussolini. Sulla freely used the powers of life and death to impose on Rome a tyranny that cost the lives and liberties and properties of thousands of his opponents.

Then, in the middle of the first century B.C., Rome found itself again in a situation of crisis from which eventually emerged Gaius Julius Caesar, the Catiline conspiracy, the struggles between and among Caesar and Crassus and Pompey, the Gallic Wars, the crossing of the Rubicon by Caesar in 49 B.C., the investiture of Caesar with the dictatorship in 49 B.C. and again in the late fall of 48 B.C., Caesar's struggle with Pompey, the battle of Pharsalus, the battles of Thapsus and Munda, Caesar's Egyptian adventure, Cleopatra, and Caesar's triumphant return to Rome.

For decades, Rome had endured internecine slaughter, civil wars, power clashes, proscriptions, murder, vengeance, empire building, riots, gang warfare, and a virtual orgy of bloodletting and violence that culminated finally in the Senate's voluntary investiture of Caesar with the dictatorship in 46 B.C., for ten years.

Note again what I have just said. The Roman Senate, without being coerced, invested Caesar with the dictatorship—an office of absolute power, traditionally limited to a period of six months but this time for ten years.

The Senate granted Caesar the right to speak his opinion first in the Senate, so that any ambitious and self-seeking member of that body could take his cue from the new master of the Roman state and trim his own opinions to the fashion of Caesar's moment.

Gaius Julius Caesar did not seize power in Rome. The Roman Senate thrust power on Caesar deliberately with forethought, with surrender, with intent to escape from responsibility. The Senate gave away power; the members—increased to 900 by Caesar—abandoned their duty as senators, and, in doing so, created in Caesar the most powerful man in the ancient world and one of the most powerful men in all history.

Then, in 44 B.C., the Roman Senate—without being coerced into doing so—dealt a death thrust to the Roman republic by declaring Julius Caesar dictator for life. Caesar's statue was placed among the statues of the ancient kings of Rome. Advance ratification was given to all of his future acts. He was above the law. His word and his command were the law, and his power and authority were absolute in all matters affecting the Roman state—financial, military, foreign, and domestic. He was king in everything but name, with more power in his hands than the kings of ancient Rome ever held.

Madam President, the day that the Roman Senate surrendered its powers and prerogatives into the hands of one man for life, was, as fate would have it, one of the most momentous and tragic days in the history of the world, for from that act and from that day ultimately flowed the assassination of Julius Caesar, and the eventual reign of Octavian, whom we know as Augustus, first of a long line of emperors. How different! Oh, how different history might have been! For from that act in 44 B.C., flowed a stream of irreversible history, on the waves of which burst forth the sorry reigns of Caligula, Nero, Vitellius, Domitian, Commodus, Caracalla, Elagabalus, Carinus, Honorius; a turbulent stream that flowed through dark centuries of intrigue and violence, conspiracy and murder; a stream which immersed in blood many of the emperors who wore the royal purple, as well as many of those who lusted after the throne. Finally, 520 years after the Senate's abject surrender of power into the hands of Caesar for life, the German Odoacer deposed the last emperor of the West—the impotent, diminutive, unfortunate Romulus Augustus.

Edward Gibbon relates that the Roman Senate then would address Zeno, the emperor in the East, urging, in the Roman Senate's name and in the name of the Roman people, that the universal seat of empire be transferred permanently, after

[ 163 ]

1,229 years, from Rome to Constantinople, thus marking the extinction of the Roman empire in the West.

Like a rock cast into a lake, the Senate's abject surrender of power to Caesar in 44 B.C. ripples and reverberates and rolls across twenty centuries of "the deep and dark blue ocean" of history.

Madam President, let us analyze the surrender of the Roman Senate's power to Caesar, and let us consider the implications of our own surrender—God forbid—to any president, of power that is unchecked by a Senate and House of Representatives.

Power is not a substance. It is not a liquid or a gas or a solid. It is not a sum of money in the bank, although money in the bank can be helpful in securing the trappings of power. It is not guns or tanks or bullets, although guns and tanks and bullets can be used to seize control. They can be the instruments of power. Power is an attitude in the minds of people. That is what power is: an attitude in the minds of people.

WITHOUT THE PEOPLES' ASSENT, NO REAL POWER

Here in the United States Senate, we can exercise power over the circumstances and events that affect people's lives, because the American people have acquiesced, through the Constitution, in our use of the throttles and levers of the engine of government to affect their lives and to make things happen by vote after vote after vote. But if tomorrow the American people ceased acquiescing through the Constitution in our use of the instruments of governmental power to affect circumstances and events in their lives, tomorrow we would descend into the abyss of oblivion as senators and as a Senate, and the people would then create a new entity or institution or organ for their governance.

When Fidel Castro came to power in Cuba, Fulgencio Batista was armed to the earlobes with rifles and machine guns and tanks and hand grenades. And yet, almost without firing a shot, Fidel Castro drove into Havana and took command, because the Cuban people had disempowered Batista and had empowered Castro by their assent and acquiescence. And the Cuban people have not yet decided to take that power back. Unfortunately, there is no legislative branch in Cuba with equal

[164]

powers and with power over the purse to challenge the powers of the dictator.

Likewise, look at our own American Revolution. In their frustration, the American patriots had disempowered the British king, George III, in the American colonies. British rule in the thirteen colonies was doomed long before Yorktown. Had the British won the military side of the war, the American patriots would never again have surrendered real power—the power to govern, based on the assent or consent of the people— into the king's hands, and the struggle would have gone on by other means until America was truly free. George Washington even declared that, were he to be defeated on the Atlantic seaboard, he planned to withdraw into present-day West Virginia, where the struggle would be continued until final victory.

Interestingly, when Lenin was informed that the Kerensky provisional government had assumed the trappings of power, Lenin was not discouraged; he was energized. Lenin knew the difference between trappings of power and real power itself. Lenin immediately set about negotiating with the German imperial government for his early return to Petrograd, as St. Petersburg was then named. Lenin realized that the fall of the czar had created a power vacuum which he, Lenin, must be ready to fill. He knew that the Russian people were desperate and that a desperate people will do anything to relieve their desperation.

Lenin knew that Kerensky had no intention of ending that desperation and that, therefore, Kerensky did not hold real power. Upon learning of the abdication of the czar, Lenin is reported to have said, "The power is just lying in the streets waiting to be picked up." And, in fact, Lenin was correct because the Russian people had never given their assent to being governed by the Kerensky government.

When Lenin arrived at the Finland Station in Petrograd from exile, after having been transported across Germany in a sealed train, the real revolution was already over. The czar was gone, and opposition to the revolution qua revolution was virtually finished. All that remained uncompleted was the consolidation of power into the hands of one revolutionary element or the other. Several groups were competing for legitimacy in the eyes of the Russian people: the Bolsheviks, the Mensheviks,

[165]

the Social Revolutionaries and others. All that was left was for the Bolsheviks to topple the straw-man provisional government, act and sound like leaders, tell the Russian people whatever they most wanted to hear, and be ready for the desperate Russian people to surrender into the Bolsheviks' hands the power to rule so that the problems of the Russian people could then be dealt with.

Unfortunately, as history has often indicated, in such instances as the rise of communism in Russia, nazism in Germany, and fascism in Italy, modern tyrannies have more frequently risen to fill power vacuums when majorities in the victim countries have abdicated their own responsibilities and surrendered power to the rising tyrant.

### WILLFUL ACCESSION OF POWER TO TYRANTS

Returning to our focus on ancient Rome, it was the Roman Senate that abdicated its responsibilities and surrendered power into the hands of a dictator, Julius Caesar, for life, without being coerced into doing so. Did Caesar intend to make himself king? Probably not. For one thing, as Roman dictator for life, Caesar possessed power far exceeding the powers of most kings in the ancient world.

Convinced that they knew the real intentions of Caesar, a small clique of aristocratic Roman senators assassinated Julius Caesar at the base of the Pompey statue in the Roman Senate on March 15, 44 B.C., as Caesar was about to speak to the Senate. These were substantial and reputable men, Brutus and others, men who believed themselves patriots who had struck down a would-be tyrant bent upon the final destruction of liberty and the Roman republic.

In truth, Brutus, Cassius, and their colleagues may have been right, for had events been allowed to take their course, the path and direction of Roman history might have been different. Had events been allowed to take their course, Brutus and Cassius might have been able to make their case against Caesar's impending tyranny, and might have received the plaudits and been hailed as the saviors of the Roman republic and Roman liberty.

Not so, however. In the role of one of history's most effective "spin doctors," Mark Antony delivered a stemwinding funeral

[166]

oration, waved the bloody toga in the faces of the mob, and set in motion another civil war which, when finished, left the Roman republic forever dead, Cicero and other visionaries executed, and dictatorial powers bestowed upon Augustus and every succeeding emperor until the fall of Constantinople to the Ottoman Turks in 1453 A.D.

Octavian was Caesar's grandnephew. Octavian did not set out to be Caesar's successor. In fact, Octavian did not know that Caesar had adopted him as his heir until the public reading of Caesar's will. Octavian was only eighteen years old at the time of Caesar's assassination and was sickly and chronically ill, hardly the attributes of a powerful leader. Indeed, there is no indication that Caesar intended Octavian to be his successor. But once Octavian had been designated as Caesar's heir, Octavian determined to assume Caesar's complete mantle, and, in part, that determination might be explained by a distinctive Roman quality. Well-born Romans aspired to public acclaim and veneration. Octavian's determination evidenced itself when it appeared that Mark Antony was ready to deny to him the legacy that Caesar had bequeathed to him, by withholding Caesar's wealth and Caesar's private papers. Combining a fortuitous destiny with a newly aroused and righteous indignation, Octavian bested all of his rivals for the pinnacle position of power in the Roman state and allowed himself to be styled "Augustus."

Augustus wanted to restore the old republic, but that was not to be. He sought to shift responsibilities from his shoulders to the Senate, but the Roman Senate preferred to toady to an imperator, an emperor, a strongman who would take charge of the national destiny. There may have been a phenomenon of man's nature at work here, for, in times of crisis, when the foundations of a society begin to shake and old certainties topple, there seems to be something in man that loves a Caesar. Something inherent, innate, and seemingly genetic yearns for the superman, a duce, a fuehrer, a caudillo, an el supremo, a strongman to whom one can turn for national salvation and security.

After ceding unlimited power to Caesar in 44 B.C., and after bestowing the same prerogatives and powers on Augustus in 27 B.C., the Roman Senate never again exercised the power and influence in the Roman state that it had enjoyed in the centuries of the old and middle republic. Although some subsequent emperors—Vespasian, for example—kept up the pretense of a partnership with the Roman Senate, the Senate never again attained to its former glory and power in the Roman state.

### THERE WAS NO INDEPENDENT SENATE

For more than one thousand years, the myth of Rome lived on in Constantinople, which was more authoritarian than Caesar or Augustus might ever have conceived. There was no independent Senate to challenge the Byzantine emperor's claim to hold authority over even the church or its theology. When Justinian murdered thirty thousand of the citizens of Constantinople in 532 A.D., during the Nika Rebellion, there was no independent Senate to challenge his right to do so. With autocrats like Justinian reigning on the Golden Horn, it was no wonder that, when the Russian people shaped their state in later centuries, no Senate was there to teach them the lessons of checks and balances and separation of powers, or of human rights or limited monarchies.

Consequently, when Ivan IV, the Terrible, massacred thousands of the inhabitants of Novgorod in 1570 A.D., no one challenged his right to exact such a price of revenge. Muscovy had no Senate.

When Peter the Great caused the deaths of thousands of workers in the swamps on which he built St. Petersburg with slave labor, there was no Senate to challenge his right to exploit his people. There was no equal legislative branch—with control over the purse—to challenge the power of Peter the Great in the Russian state.

When Lenin and Stalin created the Soviet monster of tyranny and extended its tentacles into Hungary, Poland, Czechoslovakia, the Baltic States, East Germany, and elsewhere, there was no legislative branch with power over the purse to check and balance their power.

### OUR PRESIDENCY: THE MOST POWERFUL OFFICE IN THE WORLD

Madam President, I do not contend that, by placing the line-item veto or enhanced rescissions power into the hands of any president, we would be creating, at 1600 Pennsylvania

[ 168 ]

Avenue, another Gaius Julius Caesar or another Augustus. But again and again, observers have warned against the growth in executive power. For example, until Andrew Jackson became president in 1829, after forty years under the Constitution, American presidents had vetoed only ten bills—ten bills in forty years, from the beginning of the American republic until 1829!

But during eight years in office, Andrew Jackson vetoed twelve pieces of legislation—five regular vetoes and seven pocket vetoes. Jackson's opponents nicknamed him "King Andrew I." Henry Clay referred to "this miserable, despotic veto power of the President of the United States" in a speech on the Senate floor in 1842. Clay also said:

> With the power to consummate legislation, to give vitality and vigor to every law, or to strike it dead at his pleasure, the President must ultimately become the ruler of the Nation. . . . The Government will have been transformed into an elective monarchy.

Those are the words of Henry Clay. And we should heed this warning. Were he alive today, Henry Clay would be astonished at the expansion of executive power. Let us look at the already awesome office of the presidency of the United States, even without the line-item veto or enhanced rescissions power.

The president of the United States is commander in chief over the most powerful military establishment in the history of the world, bar none. The president of the United States is our official head of state, embodying in himself far more than the roles of the queen of England or the emperor of Japan. The president is the chief executive officer of the United States government, charged with directing the official activities of a vast bureaucracy numbering into the hundreds of thousands. The president is, in fact, our supreme minister of state, setting the tone and direction of our international relations and directing the secretary of state to carry out those policies that the president deems to be appropriate. The president is also our "official face" to billions of people worldwide, his name being a household word in Buenos Aires, Rome, London, Singapore, Cairo, Tokyo, New Delhi.

[ 169 ]

In a sense, the president of the United States is also our "chief legislator." He has the power to veto, with the stroke of a pen, legislation passed by the Congress, not one member of which can ever hope to equal the prestige and power of the president—not the Speaker of the House, not the president pro tempore of the Senate, not the majority and minority leaders of either body.

Madam President, we have created in the presidency of the United States the most powerful office in the world, and the holder of that office, whether Democrat or Republican, is the most powerful man or woman in the world.

Allow me to present a contrast. On the inauguration day, March 4, 1801, at 10 o'clock in the morning, a company of Alexandria riflemen and a company of artillery paraded past Thomas Jefferson's boardinghouse, which was near here on New Jersey Avenue. About two hours later, Thomas Jefferson strolled up to Capitol Hill in the company of a few members of Congress and a few other friends. As he entered the then completed north wing of the Capitol, an artillery salute was fired. Taking his place in the crowded, small, semicircular Senate chamber, Thomas Jefferson was then sworn into office by Chief Justice John Marshall, after which Jefferson delivered a speech in a barely audible voice.

Another salute was fired outside, and the ceremony was finished. Jefferson then returned with his friends to his boardinghouse for a state dinner attended by various civilian and military leaders. That night, a scant crowd from the fledgling federal city, together with citizens from the surrounding Maryland and Virginia counties, celebrated in their fashion, and that was it! The outgoing president, John Adams, had not even been present for the inaugural ceremonies, having left town at dawn.

For two weeks, Jefferson remained at his boardinghouse: Conrad & McMunn's, it was called. There, he usually dined alone in the evening, eating whatever was the night's fare, and that without any distinction, if we are to believe Albert Gallatin's culinary judgments.

For his presidential office, Jefferson used the parlor adjoining his bedroom, and in that two weeks he did not even have

[170]

a secretary, nor did he have a single messenger to carry his statements up to Congress.

Let us compare the inauguration of 1801 with a modern inauguration, and Jefferson's initial circumstances with the situation of a president today. Several days before a modern inauguration, Hollywood stars and entertainers from the music industry will flock into town for extravagant celebrations attended by thousands. During the preinaugural period, the Washington census of stretch limousines will enjoy a decided upswing. The rentals of tuxedos and the sales of couturier-crafted gowns will skyrocket and proliferate, while the consumption of caviar and champagne will soar to dizzying new heights.

At noon on January 20, the inaugural ceremony will take place. Below the Capitol's West Front and along the Mall and Pennsylvania Avenue, a crowd of hundreds of thousands will have gathered. Hundreds of military personnel; scores of marching bands; and dozens of floats, beautifully decorated and sumptuously adorned, will participate in a vast parade that will last for hours. And then in the evening, inaugural balls will take place all over the city and last into the wee hours of the morning. Madam President, no Roman triumph, no coronation procession ever boasted such grandeur, or ever cost as much.

What are a modern president's accommodations at the White House? The president will be surrounded by dozens of servants, ready to respond to his slightest whim or sigh, while more dozens of secretaries, deputy secretaries, undersecretaries, assistant secretaries, and advisers stand ready to inundate the president with blizzards of memos. A waiting press corps with cameras and microphones at the ready will swarm into the room at the snap of his finger to carry every word that he speaks to hundreds of millions of people throughout the country and around the world.

At a moment's notice, deluxe helicopters and jet-propelled aircraft are prepared to ferry the president and his aides anywhere in the world at the cost of the government. This brings to mind a story that concerns the sense of power that a president might understandably feel. As the story goes, a White House aide entered the Oval Office to inform President Lyndon John-

[171]

son: "Mr. President, your airplane is ready," meaning Air Force One. In response, Johnson came back: "Son, they're all my airplanes"—meaning the entire inventory of the navy, army, marines, coast guard, and the air force. Now that is a sense of power!

Madam President, in a Roman triumph, a slave rode in the chariot behind the conquering general, and as the chariot moved along the streets with the procession, the slave constantly whispered into the honoree's ear: "Look behind you. See what comes after. Remember that thou, too, art mortal. Remember that thou, too, art mortal."

Madam President, in the modern Caesarism, in which the office of the presidency is becoming more and more idolized and deified, few, if any, whisper into a president's ear, either of his mortality or of the limitations on his power.

If senators give to the most powerful man in the world a line-item veto or rescissions power, we will take a great leap toward fulfilling Henry Clay's warning of an elective monarchy. Give to any president of the United States the power over the purse, and we will have proved ourselves faithless to our oath to support and defend the Constitution of the United States, just as the Roman Senate proved itself faithless to the constitution of the Roman republic when it surrendered the power over the purse to the Roman "Caesars" and the Roman emperors two thousand years ago!

I yield the floor.

*This lesson is as true today as it was two thousand years ago. Does anyone really imagine that the splendors of our capital city stand or fall with mansions, monuments, buildings, and piles of masonry? These are but bricks and mortar, lifeless things, and their collapse or restoration means little or nothing when measured on the great clock-tower of time.*

*But the survival of the American constitutional system, the foundation upon which the superstructure of the republic rests, finds its firmest support in the continued preservation of the delicate mechanism of checks and balances, separation of powers, and control of the purse, solemnly instituted by the Founding Fathers. For over two hundred years, from the beginning of the republic to this very hour, it has survived in unbroken continuity. We received it from our fathers. Let us as surely hand it on to our sons and daughters. [page 187]*

*Members of Congress Commemorate the Constitution's*
*Two-hundredth Anniversary*
*Independence Hall, Philadelphia, July 16, 1987*

# CHAPTER 14

## Constitutional Equilibrium: Mainstay of the Republic

*October 18, 1993*

Mr. BYRD. Mr. President, this is the fourteenth in my series of speeches on the history of the ancient Romans, the Roman republic, the Roman Senate, and the Roman constitutional system of checks and balances and separation of powers. When I began this series of one-hour speeches on May 5, I spoke of Montesquieu, the eminent French philosopher and author who had greatly influenced the Founding Fathers with his political theory of checks and balances and division of powers.

What influenced Montesquieu in his espousal of this political system? Montesquieu was greatly influenced by the history of the development of the English constitution and by the history of the ancient people of Rome. So impressed was Montesquieu with the Romans that he, in fact, developed and published a work of his own on the subject. Almost midway between the *Persian Letters* in 1721 and the *Spirit of the Laws* in 1748, Montesquieu published, in 1734, his *Considerations on the Causes of the Greatness of the Romans and their Decline*, which is the least well-known of the three.

I have previously stated that if we are to have a better appreciation and understanding of the U.S. Constitution—its separation of powers, and checks and balances, and the power over the purse—then we should follow in Montesquieu's tracks and study Roman history as he did, and that is what we have been doing together during these past several months.

What have we acquired to reward us for our pains? What have we learned that can be applicable to our own time, our own country, and to the political questions of today concerning checks and balances and the control over the purse? Let us see.

Mr. President, I hold that human nature is like a molecule of water. It has never changed. That which was $H_2O$ at the beginning of creation, when "the spirit of God moved upon the face of the waters," is still $H_2O$ today—two atoms of hydrogen and one atom of oxygen. And that which was human nature when Adam and Eve fell from grace, is still human nature today. It has never changed. And as human nature has not changed from the beginning, but is still motivated by the same emotions and instincts and needs and drives— love and hate and fear and greed and hunger, and so on— the history of man's actions will always have a way of repeating itself.

So, as we who live today contribute to the flow of history's unceasing stream, we will find it worth our while to examine the events of past ages, their causes and their consequences, in order that we might better understand the causes and possible consequences of the phenomena, the happenings, the events, the actions of our own life and times.

Napoleon said, "Let my son often read and reflect on history. This is the only true philosophy." We have elected, therefore, as did Montesquieu, to look to Roman history for guidance.

Roman power derived from Roman virtue, basically; in other words, from great moral qualities. The average Roman, as we have noted, was simple, steadfast, honest, courageous, law-abiding, patriotic, and reverent, and his leaders were men of uncommon dedication and acumen.

From the earliest times, the Romans possessed a profound reverence for national tradition, a firm conviction of being the special object and instrument of destiny, and a strong sense of individual responsibility and obligation to that tradition and to the fulfillment of that destiny.

ROMAN AND AMERICAN HISTORY—PARALLELS

There spring to mind several parallels between the history of the Romans and the history of our own republic, one such parallel being that the same old virtues which lent sturdiness and integrity to the early Romans, also gave stability and substance and strength and character to our own national life in the early years of its formation and development.

The Roman family was the cornerstone of the Roman social structure, and the family setting instilled in its members the self-discipline, the respect for authority, the veneration of ancestors, and the reverence for the gods that lent stability to Roman society and iron discipline to the Roman legions.

The Roman family unit was, indeed, a religious organization, a community of worship centered around the cult of the hearth and the cult of the dead. Each morning and evening, the entire family, including the slaves, offered prayers and sacrifices to the departed ancestors at the family hearth, the ever-burning flame of which symbolized both the unity and the continuity of the Roman family.

Because of their pastoral tradition, the Romans, like the Jews of the Old Testament, sacrificed animals to their gods. Reverence and the idea of obligation—inherent in the Roman conception of the relation between gods and men—inevitably developed among the Romans a strong sense of duty, a moral factor of inestimable worth.

Mr. President, we have seen that same strong tradition of family and religious values prevalent in the formation and development of our own country, from colonial times down to the mid-twentieth century. The erosion of these values in America over the last forty to fifty years has signified a decline in the moral and spiritual strength of this nation, as it did in the Roman state.

We have seen in both the Roman and American psyches a sense of Manifest Destiny, and the same urge to extend territorial frontiers. We saw in the territorial expansion of the Roman city-state what amounted to an overexpansion. We saw the drain that was placed upon Roman manpower, and the burden that was imposed upon the administration of the far-flung provinces. While, in our own case, territorial expansion has long since ceased, in recent years we have spent billions of dollars in space exploration, and today we stand in danger of overextending our international commitments and our financial capability to sustain and underwrite them.

We have also drawn Roman and American parallels in the vanishing peasantry from the land and the decline in small

[177]

family farms, the consequences of which have been increasing unemployment and crime and poverty in American cities, and a growing welfare dependence upon the state.

During the centuries of the early and middle republic, public office in Rome could be obtained only through virtue, and brought with it no pay, no salary, no benefit other than honor, and the opportunity to prove one's self worthy of being preferred for further toils on behalf of the state.

In the last century of the republic, the old citizen soldiery and the old moral structure of integrity and dedication to the cause of country gave way to greed, graft, corruption, venality, and political demagoguery, much of which we see in our own time and in our own country. The self-serving ambitions of Roman generals and politicians led to violence, civil wars, and military domination by standing armies made up of professional soldiers. In our own republic today, the military-industrial complex, against which President Eisenhower warned, can pose a threat to the system.

Thus, Mr. President, there are sundry similarities between our own history and the history of the Romans, and we senators would not find it an idle waste of time to reflect often upon those parallels.

SEPARATED AND SHARED POWERS: GUARDIAN OF LIBERTY

Now, let us turn to the consideration of the Roman political system. In the Roman republic, the political organization was complex. It was also experimental, unlike that of Lycurgus, the Spartan lawgiver of the ninth century B.C.

Lycurgus united in his constitution all of the good and distinctive features of the best governments, so that none of the principal parts should unduly grow and predominate. But inasmuch as the force of each part would be neutralized by that of the others, neither of them should prevail and outbalance another. Therefore, the constitution should remain in a state of equilibrium.

Lycurgus, foreseeing by a process of reasoning whence and how events would naturally happen, constructed his constitution untaught by adversity. But, while the Romans would achieve the same final result, according to Polybius they did not reach it by any process of reasoning but by the discipline

[178]

of many trials and struggles. And, by always choosing the best, in the light of the experience gained, they reached the same result as Lycurgus.

Let us consider the Roman system as it was seen by Polybius, the Greek historian, who lived in Rome from 168 B.C., following the battle of Pydna, until after 150 B.C., at a time when the Roman republic was at a pinnacle of majesty that excited his admiration and comment.

Polybius viewed the Roman constitution as having three elements: the executive, the Senate, and the people; with their respective shares of power in the state regulated by a scrupulous regard to equality and equilibrium.

Let us examine this separation of powers in the Roman republic as explained by Polybius. The consuls—representing the executive—were the supreme masters of the administration of the government when remaining in Rome. All of the other magistrates, except the tribunes, were under the consuls and took their orders from the consuls. The consuls brought matters before the Senate that required its deliberation, and they saw to the execution of the Senate's decrees. In matters requiring the authorization of the people, the consuls summoned the popular meetings, presented the proposals for their decision, and carried out the decrees of the majority.

In matters of war, the consuls imposed such levies upon the allies as the consuls deemed appropriate, and made up the roll for soldiers and selected those who were suitable. Consuls had absolute power to inflict punishment upon all who were under their command, and had all but absolute power in the conduct of military campaigns.

As to the Senate—we are talking about the separation of powers—as to the Senate, it had complete control over the treasury, and it regulated receipts and disbursements alike. The quaestors could not issue any public money to the various departments of the state without a decree of the Senate. The Senate controlled the money for the repair and construction of public works and public buildings throughout Italy, and this money could not be obtained by the censors, who oversaw the contracts for public works and public buildings, except by the grant of the Senate.

[179]

The Senate also had jurisdiction over all crimes in Italy requiring a public investigation, such as treason, conspiracy, poisoning, or willful murder, as well as controversies between and among allied states. Receptions for ambassadors, and matters affecting foreign states were the business of the Senate.

What part of the constitution was left to the people? The people participated in the ratification of treaties and alliances, and decided questions of war and peace. The people passed and repealed laws—subject to the Senate's veto—and bestowed public offices on the deserving, which, according to Polybius, "are the most honorable rewards for virtue."

Polybius, having described the separation of powers under the Roman constitution, how did the three parts of state check and balance each other? During the past several months, I have often referred to the various checks that the consuls, the tribunes, the Senate, and the assemblies exercised against each other. And I have paid particular attention to the veto powers of the Roman Senate and the tribunes.

Incidentally, Henry Clay, who believed that the veto power of American presidents was "despotic" and ought to be circumscribed, stated in a Senate floor speech that the veto "originated in the institution of the tribunitian power in ancient Rome," and had "been introduced from the practice under the empire into the monarchies of Europe."

Polybius explains the checks and balances of the Roman constitution, as he had observed them firsthand. Remember, he was living in Rome at the time.

What were the checks upon the consuls, the executive? The consul—whose power over the administration of the government when in the city, and over the military when in the field, appeared absolute—still had need of the support of the Senate and the people. The consul needed supplies for his legions, but without a decree of the Senate, his soldiers could be supplied with neither corn nor clothes nor pay. Moreover, all of his plans would be futile if the Senate shrank from danger, or if the Senate opposed his plans or sought to hamper them. Therefore, whether the consul could bring any undertaking to a successful conclusion depended upon the Senate, which had the absolute power, at the end of the consul's one-year term, to replace him with another consul or to extend his command.

Even to the successes of the consuls on the field of battle, the Senate had the power to add distinction and glory, or to obscure their merits, for unless the Senate concurred in recognizing the achievements of the consuls and in voting the money, there could be no celebration or public triumph.

The consuls were also obliged to court the favor of the people, so here is the check of the people against the consul, for it was the people who would ratify, or refuse to ratify, the terms of peace. But most of all, the consuls, when laying down their office at the conclusion of their one-year term, would have to give an accounting of their administration, both to the Senate and to the people. So, it was necessary that the consuls maintain the good will of both the Senate and the people.

What were the checks against the Senate? The Senate was obliged to take the multitude into account and respect the wishes of the people, for in matters directly affecting the senators—for instance, in the case of a law diminishing the Senate's traditional authority, or depriving senators of certain dignities, or even actually reducing the property of senators—in such cases, the people had the power to pass or reject the law in their Assembly.

In addition, according to Polybius, if the tribunes imposed their veto, the Senate would not only be unable to pass a decree, but could not even hold a meeting. And because the tribunes must always have a regard for the people's wishes, the Senate stood in awe of the multitude and could not neglect the feelings of the people.

But as a counterbalance, what check was there against the people? We have seen certain checks against the consuls; we have described some of the checks against the Senate. What about the people? According to Polybius, the people were far from being independent of the Senate, and were bound to take its wishes into account, both collectively and individually. For example, contracts were given out in all parts of Italy by the censors for the repair and construction of public works and public buildings. Then there was the matter of the collection of revenues from rivers and harbors and mines and lands—

everything, in a word, that came under the control of the Roman government. In all of these things, the people were engaged, either as contractors or as pledging their property as security for the contractors, or in selling supplies or making loans to the contractors, or as engaging in the work and in the employ of the contractors.

"Over all these transactions," says Polybius, "the Senate has complete control." For example, it could extend the time on a contract and thus assist the contractors; or, in the case of unforeseen accident, it could relieve the contractors of a portion of their obligation, or it could even release them altogether if they were absolutely unable to fulfill the contract. Thus, there were many ways in which the Senate could inflict great hardships upon the contractors, or, on the other hand, grant great indulgences to the contractors. But in every case, the appeal was to the Senate.

The Senate's ace card lay in its control over the purse strings. Also, the judges were selected from the Senate, at the time of Polybius, for the majority of trials in which the charges were heavy. Consequently, the people were cautious about resisting or actively opposing the will of the Senate, because they were uncertain as to when they might need the Senate's aid. For a similar reason, the people did not rashly resist the will of the consuls, because one and all might, in one way or another, become subject to the absolute power of the consuls at some point in time.

Polybius sums it up in this way:

> When any one of the three classes becomes puffed up, and manifests an inclination to be contentious and unduly encroaching, the mutual interdependency of all the three, and the possibility of the pretensions of any one being checked and thwarted by the others, must plainly check this tendency. And so the proper equilibrium is maintained by the impulsiveness of the one part being checked by its fear of the other.

Polybius' account may not have been an exact representation of the true state of the Roman system, but he was on the scene, and he was writing to tell us what he saw with his own eyes, not through the eyes of someone else. What better witness could we have?

DECLINE AND FALL OF THE ROMAN REPUBLIC

The theory of a mixed constitution—that is what ours is, a mixed constitution with checks and balances, and separation of powers—the theory of a mixed constitution had had its great measure of success in the Roman republic. It is not surprising, therefore, that the Founding Fathers of the United States should have been familiar with the works of Polybius, or that Montesquieu should have been influenced by the checks and balances and separation of powers in the Roman constitutional system, a clear and central element of which was the control over the purse, vested solely in the Senate in the heyday of the republic.

In my presentations today and heretofore on this subject, I have drawn many parallels between our own republic and the historical meanderings of that ancient republic that rose and declined along the banks of the Tiber River, a parallel which induced someone in an earlier American generation to name the tiny stream that once flowed across the present-day Mall, "Tiber Creek." It is my own sincere prayer, however, that the United States will not follow a course parallel to the Roman republic into an inexorable decline and decadence.

Mr. President, worthy scholars and thoughtful authors have exhausted rivers of ink in attempting to analyze the decline and fall of the Roman republic and the subsequent empire. Among the foremost of these author-historians is Edward Gibbon. Gibbon's *History of the Decline and Fall of the Roman Empire*, first published between 1776 and 1788, is an incontestable historical classic. No competent grasp of Roman historiography can be achieved without taking Gibbon into consideration. If senators have not read his volumes, they should read them.

Whereas Polybius wrote about the rise of the Roman republic and its greatness, Gibbon wrote about the decline and fall of the Roman empire, which followed on after the republic collapsed.

However, Gibbon outlines a case for Rome's decline and fall with which few, if any, subsequent historians will agree.

[183]

Gibbon asserts that Christianity was the cause of Rome's decline and ultimate fall.

Gibbon's assertion is not an atheist's diatribe against Christianity, as some people might assume. Gibbon's position is that Christianity's "other-worldly" orientation, its exclusivistic monotheism, its withdrawal from the larger society, its condemnation of Mediterranean culture, its fostering of monasticism, and its contemplative emphasis, when taken together, refocused the people's attention on spiritual values to the detriment of the practicality, the civic activism, and the aggressiveness that characterized and gave rise to the Roman attitude toward life.

Conversely, while Gibbon is acquainted with, and recounts most of, the evidences of Rome's decline that have nothing to do with Christianity—moral decadence, tyrannical emperors, barbarian incursions, the decline of the small family farms, the vanishing peasantry, the depletion of soils and accessible mineral resources, and the collapse of faith in the old gods— Gibbon treats these as being merely coincidental to Rome's decline, as minor distractions and sideshows around the center ring's main event, namely, Christianity's gnawing away at the empire's superstructure.

Certainly, no informed student of Roman history can ignore Gibbon's achievement, both as a historian and as an interpreter of ancient Roman civilization. But though the *Decline and Fall of the Roman Empire* is an undeniable classic, Gibbon has not written the last word on ancient Rome. Indeed, during the roughly two centuries since Gibbon wrote his masterpiece, we have witnessed a revolution in historical methodology and a reformation in our comprehension of the causes of Rome's failure. For example, the historian Will Durant, who made his political and cultural influence felt earlier in this century, broadly represents a twentieth-century perspective on the causes of Rome's decline and decay. In *The Story of Civilization*, Durant asserts that Rome was already in decline before Christianity emerged on the scene.

An eroding faith in the old Greco-Roman pantheon of deities, a decline in family life, rotting public and individual morality; the corrosion of discipline, patriotism, and the military esprit; abandonment of the land by the peasant classes, agricultural decline, and deforestation; civil wars, class struggle, international warfare, praetorian intrigues and conspiracies, assassinations, violence, and civil disorders; bureaucratic despotism, economic depression, stifling taxes, and corruption in government; mad emperors, pestilences, and plague; games and circuses, free bread, and the welfare mob—all of these wore away the moral and spiritual and social underpinnings of the Roman state, and accelerated its plunge into hopeless impotence and eventual obscurity as a military power and territorial empire.

Against such a backdrop of crises, fecklessness, and drift, Christianity served, not as a cause of decay and collapse, but as a lifeboat for a despairing populace. Rome was already a cracked shell when Christianity ascended the stage.

But, perhaps most tellingly, Durant declares: "The political causes of decay were rooted in one fact—increasing despotism destroyed the citizens' civic sense and dried up statesmanship at its source. . . . The Senate, losing ever more of its power and prestige, . . . relapsed into indolence, subservience, or venality; and the last barrier fell that might have saved the state from militarism and anarchy."

In short, Rome's fate was sealed by the one-by-one donations of power and prerogative that the Roman Senate plucked from its own quiver and voluntarily delivered into the hands, first, of Julius Caesar and then Octavian, and subsequently into the trust of the succession of Caligulas, Neros, Commoduses, and Elagabaluses who followed, until at last, the ancient and noble ideals of the Roman republic had been dissolved into the stinking brew of imperial debauchery, tyranny, megalomania, and rubble into which the Roman empire eventually sank.

At the height of the republic, the Roman Senate had been the one agency with the authority, the perspective, and the popular aura to debate, investigate, commission, and correct the problems that confronted the Roman state and its citizens. But the Senate's loss of will, and its eagerness to hand its responsibilities over to a one-man government—a man on a "white horse"—a dictator, and later an emperor, doomed Rome and predestined Rome's decline and ultimate fall.

[ 185 ]

## No Quick and Easy Solutions

Mr. President, those "political midwives" attendant on the birth of our own republic—George Washington, Alexander Hamilton, Benjamin Franklin, James Madison, James Wilson, Elbridge Gerry, Oliver Elsworth, and others—were some of the wisest men alive at that time, in this or any other country. Many had served in the Continental and Confederation Congresses and in state legislatures. All of them were experienced and reflective men.

Many of those constitutional framers were well acquainted with Cicero, Polybius, Livius, Tacitus, Suetonius, and Plutarch, and with the glories of the classical Roman republic. Those brilliant men borrowed freely from the best of ancient Rome, and purposefully and deliberately christened the upper chamber of the Congress "the Senate." Just as carefully, they set in place a system of checks and balances and separation of powers, and lodged the control of the purse in the "people's branch," to prevent the rise of a new coinage of imperial executives in the federation that they created.

Mr. President, in our own times we see the same problems, the same kinds of dilemmas that the hand of history wrote large upon Rome's slate, being written upon America's slate. In difficult times or in crises, many people grow impatient, as they grew impatient during and following the French revolution and elevated Napoleon to the emperorship; as they grew impatient during the Russian revolution and elevated Lenin to head of state; as they grew impatient in depression-era Germany and elevated Adolf Hitler to the presidency and the chancellorship; as they grew impatient in Cuba and elevated Fidel Castro to the dictatorship.

We, too, have reached a stage where we seem to remain in a state of crisis, semicrisis, or pseudocrisis, and the American people have grown impatient and are demanding solutions to serious problems—problems that do not lend themselves to easy and quick solutions. The solutions to these problems will be painful and will take time, perhaps years, to succeed.

This is not a truth that some people want to hear. Many would rather believe that quack remedies such as line-item vetoes and enhanced rescissions powers in the hands of presidents will somehow miraculously solve our current fiscal situation and eliminate our monstrous budget deficits. Of course, some people would, perhaps, prefer to abolish the Congress altogether and institute one-man government from now on. Some people have no patience with constitutions, for that matter.

Mr. President, let us learn from the pages of Rome's history. The basic lesson that we should remember for our purposes here is, that when the Roman Senate gave away its control of the purse strings, it gave away its power to check the executive. From that point on, the Senate declined and, as we have seen, it was only a matter of time. Once the mainstay was weakened, the structure crumbled and the Roman republic fell.

This lesson is as true today as it was two thousand years ago. Does anyone really imagine that the splendors of our capital city stand or fall with mansions, monuments, buildings, and piles of masonry? These are but bricks and mortar, lifeless things, and their collapse or restoration means little or nothing when measured on the great clock-tower of time.

But the survival of the American constitutional system, the foundation upon which the superstructure of the republic rests, finds its firmest support in the continued preservation of the delicate mechanism of checks and balances, separation of powers, and control of the purse, solemnly instituted by the Founding Fathers. For over two hundred years, from the beginning of the republic to this very hour, it has survived in unbroken continuity. We received it from our fathers. Let us as surely hand it on to our sons and daughters.

Mr. President, I close my series of reflections on the ancient Roman republic with the words of Daniel Webster from his speech in 1832 on the centennial anniversary of George Washington's birthday:

> Other misfortunes may be borne or their effects overcome. If disastrous war should sweep our commerce from the ocean, another generation may renew it. If it exhaust our Treasury, future industry may replenish it. If it desolate and lay waste our fields, still, under a new cultivation, they will grow green again and ripen to future harvests. It were but a trifle even if the walls of yonder Capitol were to crumble, if its lofty pillars should fall, and its gorgeous decorations

[187]

be all covered by the dust of the valley. All these might be rebuilt. But who shall reconstruct the fabric of demolished government? Who shall rear again the well-proportioned columns of constitutional liberty? Who shall frame together the skillful architecture which unites national sovereignty with State rights, individual security, and public prosperity? No. If these columns fall, they will be raised not again. Like the Colosseum and the Parthenon, they will be destined to a mournful, a melancholy immortality. Bitterer tears, however, will flow over them than were ever shed over the monuments of Roman or Grecian art. For they will be the remnants of a more glorious edifice than Greece or Rome ever saw: the edifice of constitutional American liberty.

Mr. President, I thank the Chair and I thank all senators.

*Remove not the ancient landmark, which thy fathers have set.*
Proverbs 22:28

☙❧

*Except the Lord build the house, they labour in vain that build it: except the Lord keep the city, the watchman waketh but in vain.*
Psalm 127:1

[189]